PETERLOO MASSACRE 1819

Philip G, McKeiver
B.A., M. Litt., M. A. Hons.

Advance Press
Manchester

A Victorian View of the 15th Hussars charging the Peterloo Crowd.

For my Grandmother Dorothy Jones and Great Grandmother Penelope Ridings.

ISBN 978-0-9554663-1-1

Printed and bound in Great Britain by
Albany Press
Levenshulme, Manchester

First published in the UK in 2009 by

Advance Press
Suite 191, 792 Wilmslow Road, Didsbury, Manchester, M20 6UG

Preface

My interest in Peterloo was aroused during my research into my family history and discovering that one of my relatives led one of the contingents of Radical Reformers to the meeting in 1819. I found that almost every book dealing with English history during the post-Napoleonic period, have at least one paragraph describing the Peterloo Massacre which occurred on 16th August 1819 at St Peter's Field, in Manchester. There have also been a number of historical studies. Therefore the purpose of this book is to examine the scholarship on this very controversial historical topic.

Clear-headed assessments in the aftermath of Peterloo have been a long time coming. Although it became known as the Peterloo Massacre, the events in and around St. Peter's Field on 16th August 1819 were regarded by both sides with a great deal of passion. At the time the Peterloo Massacre divided English society as a whole, with petitions and mass meetings being organised *for* and *against* the position taken by the Manchester authorities.[1] As Philip Lawson emphasises contention lies at the heart of Peterloo because 'one side argues that the reformers went too far in their protest or demonstration at St Peter's Field and that in the aftermath of Peterloo, support for the established order was reaffirmed by the mass of the population' and 'on the other side exists the view that a legitimate movement of popular constitutionalism ended in a massacre, betrayed on all sides by middle-class equivocation and a corrupt and repressive political system.'[2]

---

[1] W. A. Speck, *A Concise History of Britain 1707-1975*, Cambridge, (1995), p. 67.
[2] Philip Lawson, 'Reassessing Peterloo,' *History Today*, March, (1988), pp. 24-25.

Although this book is essentially a historiographical study, and solidly based on the historiographical evidence, I have used relevant primary sources and eyewitness accounts. Some of these accounts appear in the *Inquest on the Body of John Lees, the Whole proceedings before the Coroner's Inquest at Oldham on the body of John Lees, who died of sabre wounds at Manchester.* Edited by Joseph A. Dowling, London, (1820), and in H.W.C. Davis, *Lancashire Reformers 1816-1817*, reprinted from *The Bulletin of the John Rylands Library*, Vol. 10. No.1, January, (1926). In addition I have used F.A. Bruton's study *Three Accounts of Peterloo by Eyewitnesses, Bishop Stanley, Lord Hylton, and Benjamin Smith,* Manchester, (1921), which is considered as a standard modern authority. Other relevant primary accounts appear in Samuel Bamford's, *Passages in the Life of a Radical,* Manchester, (1841), in Archibald Prentice, *Historical Sketches and Personal Recollections of Manchester, Intended to Illustrate the Progress of Public Opinion from 1792 to 1832,* Manchester, (1851), and other contemporary works have also been presented. I have also relied on the more recent research of Professor Michael Bush, *The Casualties of Peterloo,* Manchester, (2005), in which he has published detailed lists of every known casualty of *Peterloo* and his analysis of these lists establishes the exact scale and nature of the Peterloo Massacre.

Acknowledgments

My grateful thanks to the staff at the University of Manchester, John Ryland's Library, and Chetham's Library, Manchester. The Working-class Movement Library, Salford, and the Local Studies Unit of the Manchester Central Library, also known as the Round Library, located in what is now known as St Peter's Square, who have responded to my requests with great efficiency. I am especially grateful to my good friends Professor Patrick Gallagher, Anthony Goulding B.Sc., University College, Cardiff and Kieran Power B.A., University of Warwick, for their advice and input in the final planning stages of this book.

As far as possible, modern spelling has been used throughout, although printed primary sources appear in their original form.

Map

List of Illustrations

The picture on the front cover depicts William Hone's savage comment on the massacre announcing the erection of a mock-monument-with trooper trampling woman and child on a base of skulls, in commemoration of the achievements of the Manchester Yeomanry Cavalry.

A Victorian View of the 15th Hussars charging the Peterloo Crowd. (Inner Cover)

CONTENTS

Biographical Sketches[3]

Any assessment of the political background to Peterloo must begin with a series of biographical sketches.

Baines, Edward, Reporter for the *Leeds Mercury* at Peterloo.

Bagguley, John, a leading Stockport Radical and promoter of the March o f the Blanketeers in 1817.

Bamford, Samuel, (1788-1872) the celebrated weaver-poet from Middleton, author of *Passages in the Life of a Radical*, in which he gave his own account of Peterloo. He was an active member in the Hampden Club and although he disapproved of the *Blanketeers* meeting, was nevertheless arrested by the authorities and sent to London for questioning, but was later released. At Peterloo he led the Middleton contingent to Peterloo and was arrested for his part in the meeting.

Birley, Captain Hugh Hornby, a wealthy manufacturer who owned a mill in Oxford Road. He was the second officer-in-charge of the Manchester and Salford Yeomanry on 16th August 1819 who led the charge of the yeomanry into the crowd at Peterloo. Afterwards he became a magistrate and the founder of the Manchester Chamber of Commerce. He was later appointed Deputy Lieutenant of the County Palatine of Lancashire.

Burdett, Sir Francis, was recognised as the leader of the Radicals in the House of Commons. He introduced motions for parliamentary reform and supported all attempts to expose corruption in government circles. In 1819, he was responsible for leading the campaign to press for an independent inquiry into the Peterloo Massacre.

---

[3] These brief biographical sketches are based on the relevant sections of *The Concise Dictionary of National Biography*, Oxford, (1992); Donald Read, *Peterloo, The "Massacre" and its Background*, Manchester, (1957), and on research material in subsequent chapters.

Byng, General Sir John, Commander of the Northern District in 1819. In later life he became the Whig, M.P. for Poole.

Carlile, Richard, (1790-1843), a Devonshire shoemakers son, journeyman, tinsmith and mechanic in London in 1813. Later in 1818 he published Thomas Paine's *The Rights of Man.* He escaped from the hustings at Peterloo and hid in a house nearby. Later in 1819 he was prosecuted for publishing *The Rights of Man* and was imprisoned at Dorchester Gaol 1819-1825. He later became the proprietor of Sherwin's, *Political Register* changing its name to the *Republican* and editing twelve volumes whilst still in prison. He was finally released in 1825.

Cartwright, Major, John, formed the first Hampden Club in 1812. He then toured the country encouraging other parliamentary reformers to follow his example. His main objective was to unite middle-class moderates with radical members of the working-class. This frightened the authorities and led to his arrest at Huddersfield in 1813 and 1815. He recruited John Knight who founded the first Hampden Club in Lancashire and who invited him to speak at the Peterloo meeting in 1819 but he was unable to attend.

Castlereagh, Viscount Stewart, Robert, Leader of the House of Commons in Lord Liverpool's government.

Cobbett, William, In 1802 he founded his newspaper *The Political Register.* To begin, with Cobbett supported the Tory Government but gradually became a Radical. By 1806 he was a strong advocate of parliamentary reform largely due to his unsuccessful attempt to be elected as M.P. for Honiton, which convinced him of the unfairness of Rotton Boroughs. However, after *Habeas Corpus* was suspended and suspecting he was in t the firing line for prosecution by the government, he migrated to America.

Drummond, Samuel, a leading Stockport Radical and promoter of the March of the Blanketeers in 1817.

Entwistle, John, Member of the Select Committee of Magistrates.

Ethelstone, Reverend, Charles, Wickstead, (1767-1830), who was a Manchester Magistrate, although not a member of the Special Committee of Magistrates he signed the warrant for the arrest of the speakers and read the Riot Act at Peterloo.

Fielden, Mr, a member of the Select Committee of Magistrates.

Fletcher, Colonel Ralph, Member of the Select Committee of Magistrates.

George, III, King from 1760-1820.

Gregg, Robert, Hyde, the owner of Quarry Bank Mill in Styal, Cheshire near Manchester. Along with his wife's cousin, Francis Philips witnessed the Peterloo Massacre in 1819. Gregg later gave evidence in defence of the Radicals.

Harrison, Reverend, Joseph, was a local Nonconformist Preacher. His politico-religious sermons became regular features of Stockport Radicalism. As a result of three speeches that he made, one on 15th August 1819, the other on 18th December 1819 and for a speech he made at Stockport on 28th June 1820, he was sentenced to three and a half years imprisonment.

Hay, Reverend William, Robert, (1761-1839), Clerical Magistrate at the time of Peterloo. Later appointed vicar of Rochdale in 1820, but also served as a Clerical Magistrate and until 1823 as the Stipendiary Chairman of the Salford Quarter Sessions.

Healey, Dr, (1780-1830), A leading Radical Reformer and in 1819, he led the Saddleworth, Lees, and Mossley Union contingent to Peterloo headed by a black flag. This caused great consternation in local 'loyalist' circles. It was chiefly because of this that he was arrested at the meeting. His wife was Secretary to the Manchester Female Reformers and the sub editor of the *Manchester Observer.*

Hobhouse, Henry, (1776-1904), Permanent under-secretary for the Home Office in Lord Liverpool's Government and keeper of state papers, 1817-1827.

Hone, William, Radical, illustrator, caricaturist and author of *The Political House that Jack Built,* (1819). Hone's pamphlets attacking George IV forced the king to attempt to bribe him.

Hulton, William, (1787-1864), The Chairman of the Special Committee of Lancashire and Cheshire Magistrates formed in July 1819.

Hunt, Henry, (1773-1835), known as Orator Hunt, was the chief speaker at Peterloo. In 1817 he first came into contact with Lancashire Radicalism through the Hampden Club movement. His capacity as an orator soon won him a large personal following throughout the country and especially in Lancashire. He was found guilty of seditious assembly and sentenced to two and a half years imprisonment. In 1830 he was elected as the M.P. for Preston.

Johnson, John, a leading Stockport Radical and promoter of the March of the Blanketeers in 1817.

Johnson, Joseph, (1791-1872), the most active local radical, organiser behind the Peterloo meeting. In June 1818 he became the part-owner of the Radical local newspaper the *Manchester*

Observer. It was about this time also that he became secretary of the Manchester *Patriotic Union Society*, and was responsible for inviting Orator Hunt to speak at the Peterloo meeting.

Jolliffe, Lieutenant William, a nineteen-year old officer in the 15th Hussars on St Peter's Field, whose eyewitness account was later published in Pellew's *Life of Sidmouth* which was printed in Bruton 1921.

Knight, John, (1763-1838), a small-scale Manchester cotton manufacturer and a well established figure in local radical circles. As early as 1811 he had published a reform pamphlet, and in 1812 he was arrested for administering illegal oaths to a committee formed to prepare a reform address to the Prince Regent.

Lord Liverpool, Robert, Banks, Jenkinson, (1770-1828), Tory Prime Minister 1812-1827.

L'Estrange, Lieutenant-Colonel, George, the military commander in Manchester 1819 under Major-General Sir John Byng, commander of the northern district.

Mallory, Reverend, A member of the Select Committee of Magistrates.

Marriott, Mr, a member of the Select Committee of Magistrates.

Marsh, Richard, a member of the Select Committee of Magistrates.

Nadin, Joseph, (1765-1884), The Deputy Chief Constable of Manchester during and following Peterloo.

Norris, James, a Barrister, large landowner and a member of the Select Committee of Magistrates.

Oliver, William, one of the most active and energetic secret agents of Lord Liverpool's' Government, nick named 'Oliver the Spy.'

Paine, Thomas, author of *The Rights of Man.*

Pitt, William, British Tory Prime Minister and 1st Earl of Chatham, who died in 1812 and was succeeded by Lord Liverpool.

Philips, Francis, was a cotton manufacturer and a prominent member of the Pitt Club and Tory party. Soon after Peterloo, Philips published *An Exposure of the Calumnies circulated by the Enemies of Social Order and reiterated by their abettors Against the Magistrates and Yeomanry Cavalry of Manchester and Salford,* (1819), defending the behaviour of the Manchester magistrates and the Cavalry at Peterloo.

Prentice, Archibald, (1792-1857), watched the start of the meeting in St. Peter's Field, from the window of a friend's house in Mosley Street. He helped to found the Radical newspaper the *Manchester Gazette* in 1821 which was incorporated with the *Manchester Times* in 1828. He later became the sole manager of this paper. Some years later Prentice published his book, *Historical Sketches and Personal Recollections of Manchester*, (1851).

Prince Regent, stood-in for George III who in 1811 had lost his mind. He later became George IV.

Redford, Thomas, Radical plaintiff in *Redford v Birley*, April, 1822.

Ridings, Elijah, (1802-1872), Manchester working-class poet, weaver and bookseller, Peterloo veteran, anti Corn Law campaigner and Chartist. In 1819, being then 17 years of age, he was appointed leader of a section of parliamentary reformers at Newton Heath and Miles Platting on the memorable march to Peterloo and narrowly escaped being trampled by Yeomanry horses with the help of an officer of the 15th Hussars.

Saxton, John, Assistant Editor of the *Manchester Observer* and a radical orator who was arrested on the hustings on 16th August but later acquitted at his trial at York.

Sidmouth, Addington, Henry, (1757-1844), 1st Viscount, was the Home Secretary in Lord Liverpool's Cabinet.

Smith, John, Reporter from the *Liverpool Mercury* at Peterloo.

Stanley, Reverend, Edward, (1779-1849), Formerly the Rector of Alderly and later Bishop of Norwich, whose eyewitness account of the scene at Peterloo and his evidence in *Redford v Birley* supported the radical accounts.

Swift, George, Young Radical Reformer arrested on the hustings along with Henry Hunt. He was placed on trial with Hunt but acquitted of all charges.

Sylvester, J, Member of the Select Committee of Magistrates.

Taylor, John, Edward, Founder of *The Manchester Guardian,* who along with John Tyas, a correspondent from *The Times* witnessed the events at Peterloo from the hustings.

Tatton, Thomas, W, Member of the Select Committee of Magistrates.

Teesdale, Colonel, Commander of the Kings' Dragoon Guards at the Blanketeers meeting held in St Peter's Field in 1817.

Thistlewood, Arthur, Radical who planned the Cato Street Conspiracy in 1820 and was hanged on the 1st May 1820 along with four of his accomplices.

Trafford, Major Thomas, Joseph, manufacturer and the Senior Officer commanding the Manchester and Salford Yeomanry Cavalry who managed to escape the criticism directed at Captain Hugh Hornby Birley, his second in command.

Trafford, Trafford, one of the magistrates who accompanied Lieutenant L'Estrange onto St Peter's Field on 16th August, 1819.

Tyas, John, London reporter for *The Times* newspaper at Peterloo who was arrested on the hustings along with Hunt.

Walker, Thomas, A rich Unitarian cotton merchant who established the *Manchester Constitutional Society* in October, 1790.

Wolseley, Sir Charles, (1769-1846), like Hunt he was more than a local leader. He was one of the founders of the Hampden Club and was elected 'Legislatorial Attorney' for Birmingham at a meeting on 12th July 1819. He was imprisoned for eighteen months for a violent speech he made at Stockport along with Harrison on 28th June 1819. After his release he continued to play an active part in Radical affairs.

Wright, Mr, a member of the Select Committee of Magistrates.

Wroe, James, (1788-1844), Between June 1819 and February 1820 he was the editor of the *Manchester Observer*. He was hounded by the Manchester local authorities and indicted for seditious publications and distribution. In February 1820 poverty-stricken by the cost of litigation, he was forced to give up the *Manchester Observer*. Nevertheless, he maintained his commitment to the Reform Movement throughout the 1820's and 1830's. In 1838 he was elected as one of Manchester's delegates to the first Chartist National Convention.

Wooler, Thomas, Jonathan, The editor of the Radical newspaper the *Black Dwarf.*

William Hulton, Chairman of the Select Committee of
Magistrates.
Manchester Library and Information Service: Manchester Archives and Local Studies

Chapter One

Historical Background to Peterloo

By 1819 Manchester had grown into England's second largest city, and the world's first industrial city. Its status remained that of a medieval market town owned by the Mosley family. It had no Member for Parliament, and magistrates from the Counties Palatine of Lancaster and Chester were empowered to take control in times of unrest. Before August 16th a Select Committee of Magistrates had already assumed control of the town, which was regarded by Lord Liverpool's administration as the most troublesome, turbulent, seditious, and wicked area in the country. [Joyce Marlow] [4]

A few days after the meeting the *Manchester Observer* coined the name Peterloo, associating it in mockery with Napoleons defeat at the Battle of Waterloo which had taken place four years earlier. Thus: the name *Peterloo* and even the *Peterloo Massacre* became a powerful and emotive symbol for generations in the shaping of political opinion.[5] In the words of Simon Schama, 'There was something evil about Peterloo, which for many mocked the pretension of the government to be upholding British traditions against innovation. Peterloo was not, the critics believed, a British event.' [6]

---

[4] Joyce Marlow, 'The Day of Peterloo,' *Manchester Regional History Review*, Vol. iii, (1989), p. 3.
[5] Harry Horton, *Peterloo, 1819 A Portfolio of Contemporary Documents*, Manchester Libraries Committee, (1969), p. 3.
[6] Simon Schama, *Britain The Fate of Empire 1776-2000*, London, (2002), p. 134.

Although the name Peterloo is now well-known its memory has faded over the generations.[7] However, there is no doubt that Peterloo was a major event in British history, and the most important day in Manchester's political history.[8] It was also one of the bloodiest days in Manchester's history which occurred at St Peter's Field where the Free Trade Hall stands today, and close to St. Peter's Square.[9] Almost every writer dealing with the post-Napoleonic period of British history has touched on this controversial topic with the exception of Winston Churchill, who in *A History of English Speaking Peoples* did not mention it at all. However, historians generally agree that a repressive Government and an equally repressive Select Committee of Magistrates brutally dispersed a peaceful Radical Reform meeting with tragic results. [10]

To place the period in historical context there is no doubt that, the great technical advances of the Industrial Revolution were certainly not accompanied by any comparable improvements in British society as a whole. A few men of 'humble birth' were enabled to make fortunes beyond their wildest dreams which had previously not been possible. However, in the words of Chris Aspin 'the headlong pursuit of wealth dragged many thousands into misery and degradation. Government, badly informed and often misled about the state of the manufacturing districts, reacted to the people's unrest with exaggerated alarm and too often introduced measures that added fuel to the fire beneath the Lancashire cauldron, which for more than half a

[7] Robert Reid, *The Peterloo Massacre*, London, (1989), p. xiii.
[8] Alan, Kidd, *Manchester*, (third edition), Edinburgh, (2002), p. 90.
[9] Tom Waghorn, 'Killing Field,' in Horrock's Paul, (ed.), *The Making of Manchester*, (1999), p. 12.
[10] Robert Warmsley, *Peterloo: The Case Re-opened*, Manchester, (1969), p. 21.

century simmered, and from time to time boiled over, with bitter passions of class hatred.'[11]

In 1819 Manchester was only one of several industrial centres where unenfranchised working men had organised themselves into clubs to discuss political topics, to make plans for a constitutional reform of Parliament and to hasten this reform by means of demonstrations which were intended to persuade the ruling class. The industrial towns in Lancashire looked to Manchester to take the lead. Here the reform movement was more vigorous but was also more carefully watched by the local magistrates.[12]

By 1819, the manufacturing and selling of cotton was the main occupation of the people of Manchester and surrounding towns. Raw cotton arrived at Liverpool from America, was sold by dealers to Manchester merchants who then passed it on to master spinners. The two basic manufacturing processes were the spinning into yarn and weaving into cloth. By this time spinning was mainly done in mills with new machinery whilst the weaving process was still largely carried out by handloom weavers working from home.[13]

Throughout the Napoleonic Wars migrant workers had flocked into Manchester not only from Lancashire, but from all counties of England, Wales, Scotland and Ireland.[14] Because of the increasing demand for children in the cotton trade, many large families were included among the migrant workers.[15] All these

---

[11] Chris Aspin, *The First Industrial Society, Lancashire, 1750-1850*, Oxford, (1995), p. 49.

[12] H. W. C. Davis, *Lancashire Reformers, 1816-1817*, London, (1926), Reprinted from 'The Bulletin of the John Rylands Library,' Vol. 10, No. I, January, (1926)

[13] Donald Read, *Peterloo: The 'Massacre' and its Background*, Manchester, (1958), p. 5.

[14] Asa Briggs, *Victorian Cities*, Harmondsworth, (1971), p. 88.

[15] Neil J. Smelser, *Social Change in the Industrial Revolution: An Application of Theory to the Lancashire Cotton Industry 1770-1840*, London, (1972), p. 188.

people were poverty-stricken and had come to settle in Manchester to benefit from the work the new cotton industry provided.[16]

As early as 1815, over 24,000 workers were employed in the sixty spinning mills located in the Manchester region. Although ninety per cent of spinning was carried out in mills other spinners operated from home.[17] Manchester is also believed to have had no less than 10,000 silk weavers in 1815 and over the following decade the silk trade increased dramatically. Most of the silk weavers were recruited from the skilled workers in the cotton trade in Manchester itself but most were recruited from Macclesfield.[18]

The cotton trade created modern Manchester along with a small privileged middle-class and a large group of working-class who were condemned to a life of hardship. There was no doubt that the cotton industry was responsible for the increasing growth and wealth of the town. It was not long before Manchester became one of the commercial capitals of Europe long before it became an incorporated town in 1838. On the one hand Manchester's progress was reflected by the newness of its buildings and on the other hand by its squalor. However, most of the buildings in Manchester were already blackened with smoke by the beginning of the nineteenth century. A visitor from Rotherham declared as early as 1808:

---

[16] Reid, *op. cit.*, p. 5.

[17] Marlow, *op. cit.*, pp. 16-17.

[18] W. H. Thomson, *History of Manchester to 1852*, Altrincham, (1966), p. 281.

The town is abominably filthy, and the Steam Engine is pestiferous, the Dye houses noisome and offensive, and the water of the river as black as ink or the Stygian lake.[19]

From the late 1780s up until the first census of 1801 Manchester's population had risen from 40,000 to over 70,000. The population had grown to 108,000 in 1821, and 142,000 by 1831.[20] The surrounding towns like Ashton, Bolton, Blackburn, Rochdale and Stockport had also grown at the same alarming rate.[21] After visiting Manchester Engels described the working conditions in one of the cotton mills by the 1840's as follows:

In the cotton and flax spinning mills there are many rooms in which the air is filled with fluff and dust...The operative of course had no choice in the matter...The usual consequences of inhaling factory dust are the spitting of blood, heavy, noisy breathing, pains in the chest, coughing and sleeplessness...Accidents occur to operatives who work in rooms crammed full of machinery...The most common injury is the loss of a joint of the finger...In Manchester one sees not only numerous cripples, but also plenty of workers who have lost the whole or part of an arm, leg or foot.[22]

It must be remembered that towards the end of the eighteenth century enlightened thinkers were writing about social equality, the will of the majority and the end of the feudal system which was still binding the rural population of Europe to its aristocratic

---

[19] Briggs, *op. cit.*, pp. 88-89.
[20] Horton, *op. cit.*, p. 3.
[21] Briggs, *op. cit.*, p. 89.
[22]Tristram Hunt, 'No Marx without Engels,' *History Today*, Vol. 59, April, (2009), p. 51.

rulers. These writers argued that power should not be simply vested in aristocratic elite, the Church or even the mercantile class but be shared by the people.[23] However, the aristocracy in England still believed that the majority of the middle-class as well as the poor should be excluded from the 'sacred circle of the parliamentary Constitution.'[24]

Throughout the last years of George III's reign, national consciousness had been promoted through public celebrations of 'loyalty' and 'royalty' by spectacular military parades to elicit popular support for the existing order, the Church and King.[25] However, things began to change in England and in Manchester in particular when in 1790 two new political constitutional reform societies were established, and partisan opinions and prejudices grew around them. As early as March 1790, the dominant Anglican-Tory oligarchy in Manchester established *The Church and King Club*, to celebrate the successful defence of the Test and Corporation Acts which became the focus for organised campaigns against constitutional reformers. Its motto and toast of 'Church and King, and down with the Rump,' stemmed from earlier confrontations within the Manchester middle-class.[26]

During October 1790 Thomas Walker, a Unitarian cotton manufacturer, established a rival liberal association, the Manchester Constitutional Society. Between May and June of 1792 two more radical clubs were established, one the Patriotic and the other the Constitutional Society, whose members were

---

[23] Angus Konstam, *Historical Atlas of The Napoleonic Era*, London, (2003), p. 8.
[24] H.A.L. Fisher, *A History of Europe: From the Early 18th Century to 1935*, Glasgow, (1979), p. 789.
[25] John Belchem, 'Manchester, Peterloo and The Radical Challenge,' *Manchester Regional History Review*, Vol. iii, (1989), p. 9.
[26] John K, Walton, *Lancashire A Social History, 1558-1939*, Manchester, (1987), p. 136.

largely weavers, labourers and journeymen, [tradesmen]. Both of these clubs were committed to peaceful reforms although still acting under the patronage of Thomas Walker's society. [27] In effect the Manchester Constitutional Society of 1790-1793 was a middle-class organisation though it had satellite clubs of working-class reformers.[28]

In May of 1792, the Constitutional Society issued a declaration that Members of Parliament should owe their seats to the *free suffrage* of the people. However, within a week the Government issued a proclamation against these 'wicked and seditious writings.' [29] In June 1792, following a loyalist meeting to celebrate the King's birthday, the loyalist crowd attacked two 'Dissenting chapels, one of them the Unitarian chapel in Mosley Street.' However, the local authorities made no attempt to intervene. Instead, the loyalist propaganda war against the Constitutional Society and Thomas Walker gained momentum.[30] There is no doubt that loyalist political societies played an important role in counteracting the influence of Radicalism. [31]

By September 1792, a total of 186 innkeepers and publicans in Manchester had signed a declaration of loyalty and banned members of reformer clubs from entering their public houses. Although it was rumoured at the time, that some had had their licences threatened beforehand by the local authorities. Further radical activity in Manchester sparked a spate of 'loyalist-inspired mob violence.' For example in December 1792, The

[27] Michael, J. Turner, *Reform and Respectability, The Making of a Middle-Class Liberalism in 19th Century Manchester*, Manchester, (1995), pp. 39-41.
[28] Davis, *op. cit.*, p. 4.
[29] Thomson, *op. cit.*, p. 246.
[30] Turner, *op. cit.*, p. 42-43.
[31] Eric J. Evans, *The Forging of The Modern State, Early Industrial Britain 1783-1870*, London, (1996), p. 88.

Manchester Herald offices were attacked, along with Walkers' house where the Reformation Society had been meeting. Again the authorities did nothing to stop the offenders. As a precaution Walker collected firearms to defend himself against possible future attacks. This soon came to the notice of the authorities and he was arrested. This led to a trial at the Lancaster Assizes on a trumped up charge to 'overthrow the Constitution and Government and to aid and assist the French.' Although Walker was acquitted, he was financially ruined by the cost of the trial. His trial also had the effect of frightening many reformers into keeping quiet or going underground.[32]

Between 1792 and 1815, no less than 155 military barracks were constructed to accommodate the army. Most of these were strategically placed in the 'disaffected' districts of the Midlands, the North, and especially in Manchester and her surrounding towns. In the words of E.P. Thompson: 'England until 1792 had been governed by consent and deference supplemented by the gallows and the Church and King mob.' [33]

After 1795 public agitation for reform had many problems to overcome. Largely due to the repressive legislation passed by William Pitt's Tory government, and the waves of loyalist sentiment which were aroused.[34] One of the most permanent results of reform agitation in Manchester was the consolidation of the loyalists who formed the *Manchester Association for Preserving Liberty, Order and Property* who worked very closely with the local authorities. The magistrates and the town officers were some of its leading members.[35]

---

[32]Turner, *op. cit.*, pp. 42-43.
[33] E. P. Thompson, *The Making of the English Working Class*, London, (1991), p. 663.
[34] J.R. Dinwiddy, *From Luddism to the First Reform Bill: Reform in England 1810-1832*, Oxford, (1986), p. 19.
[35]Turner, *op. cit.*, pp. 42-43.

However, Radicalism was silenced by the Government in 1795 with relative ease. Once radical societies had no response to their arguments on reform they had no other way of persuading a Parliament made up of property owners who were united in their belief that their patrimony was threatened. [36]

As early as 1800, the Government had passed the Combination Acts to prevent workers from forming organisations to fight for improved conditions.[37] These Acts were passed at the request of the employers in the trades concerned.[38] In addition the magistrates were able to lock up men and women under the Acts, which they frequently did. The Combination Acts made it practically impossible for workers to try to improve their lot without risking prosecution and imprisonment. By using the Combination Acts against workers and allowing employers to combine openly whenever they pleased, the magistrates were able to put the majority of the working-class completely under the control of their employers.[39] However, in spite of the Combination Acts the unions of cotton spinners still maintained an underground existence.[40]

Because their position was unchallenged, the wealthy classes fell into the habit of believing that all national and economic problems were in keeping with their own self interest. It seemed that the law of the land existed for no other purpose than the control and punishment of the working-class.[41] There is no doubt the Home Secretary, Lord Sidmouth, with his unbending

---

[36] Evans, *op. cit.*, p. 92.
[37] Lloyd Evans and Philip Pledger, *Triumph and Tribulation, A Political and Social History of Britain Since 1815*, Melbourne, (1972), p. 9.
[38] A. Aspinall, *The Early English Trade Unions*, London, (1949), p. x.
[39] Thomson, *op. cit.*, p. 286.
[40] Davis, *op. cit.*, p. 4.
[41] Trevelyan, *op. cit.*, p. 143.

reverence for law and order was responsible for maintaining this policy.[42]

Despite the severity of Government measures, between 1800 and 1815, the discontent of the masses had frequently erupted in agitation in the form of strikes, rioting and machine breaking.[43] Following the closure of American trade early in 1811 and after the introduction of new machinery into the various mills most of the framework knitters were unemployed causing widespread poverty. This state of affairs in the East Midlands was responsible for the start of the Luddite movement. The Luddite movement erupted when bands of textile workers began to destroy machinery in textile mills which they blamed for the loss of their jobs. The Luddites as they were known wore masks after dark and their leader real or imagined was known as General Ludd. [44]

The Prime Minister William Pitt died in 1812 and was succeeded by Lord Liverpool. His government believed Luddism was part of a widespread conspiracy plotting revolution. The conspiracy was a myth and most of the information regarding revolutionary activity was invented by government spies and *agents provocateurs*, who deliberately stirred up risings to accumulate evidence.[45] In an attempt to smash the rising the government introduced the Frame Breaking Act in 1811 which imposed the death penalty for machine breaking.[46] In fact the Luddite movement was largely non-political and not part of a revolutionary plot. Generally machine

---

[42] Reid, *op. cit.*, pp. 24-25.

[43] Evans and Pledger, *op. cit.*, p. 9.

[44] Donald Read, *The English Provinces c. 1760-1960, a study in influence*, London, (1964), pp. 61-62.

[45] C. P. Hill, *British Economic and Social History 1700-1982*, London, (1986), p. 68.

[46] Aspin, *op. cit.*, p. 102.

breaking was down to a few bands of machine breakers sometimes supported by spontaneously assembled mobs. Although early agitation was confined to Nottinghamshire by the end of 1811 it had spread to Yorkshire, Derbyshire and finally to Lancashire.[47]

Altogether no less than 12,000 troops were employed by the government in their attempts to put down the Luddites disturbances.[48] Finally the government took ruthless measures rounding up large numbers of Luddites leading to a mass trial at York in 1813. Twenty men were hanged including a boy of 16 years who had been a look-out whilst his brothers were setting fire to a Lancashire mill. Most of the others convicted of offences were transported to Australia for life. There is no doubt that for the government the Luddite movement was a warning of horrors to come.[49] As it happens however, workers in Lancashire and what can be described as the other Luddite counties gave up their old activities to embrace popular radicalism as a way of looking for 'democratic control of the state and the economy' to improve their lot.[50]

It must also be remembered that between 1793 and 1815 Britain was almost continuously at war with France.[51] This had cost the Government £800 million. In 1815 the last year of the war had cost Britain £81 million, of which £27 million had been raised by a loan. Nevertheless, on Wellington's triumphant return to London after defeating Napoleon at Waterloo,

---

[47] Read, *op. cit.*, p. 62. *English Provinces*
[48] Frank Ongley Darvall, *Popular Disturbances and Public Disorder in Regency England*, London, (1934), p. 1.
[49] Hill, *op. cit.*, p. 68.
[50] Belchem, *op. cit.*, p. 9.
[51] Hill, *op. cit.*, p. 61.

a grateful Parliament rewarded him with £200,000. [52] Liberal allowances were also paid to the relatives of the Ministers in government and to the Commanding Officers.[53] In contrast, the veterans who had fought on the battlefield at Waterloo, returned to the manufacturing towns like Manchester and other towns in the north of England largely unpaid to face unemployment.[54]

By 1815 the parliamentary system in Britain had almost gone back to the Middle Ages, certainly not reflecting the needs of the rapidly changing society. Altogether there were '658 MPs in the House of Commons' but how they were elected was to come under close scrutiny. This is largely because there were no independent MPs representing the new expanding industrial centres like Manchester.[55] The working-classes blamed their misery on misgovernment and the fact that they had no proper representation in Parliament to redress their grievances. They could see Manchester, Salford, Bolton, Blackburn, Rochdale, Bury, Ashton-under-Lyne, Oldham, and Stockport had no members in parliament, whilst a host of small villages with only a few inhabitants often had two, MPs.[56]

To make matters worse for the working-classes, by 1819 the administration of justice in Manchester was still in the hands of a few county magistrates. There were about eighteen magistrates, including a chief stipendiary magistrate. On the other hand the administration of local poor relief and the payment of the Police were in the hands of the churchwardens and overseers of the poor. All branches of local government

---

[52] Reid, *op. cit.*, pp. 20-21.
[53] Thompson, *op. cit.*, p. 663.
[54] Reid, *op. cit.*, pp. 20-21.
[55] Roy Strong, *The Story of Britain*, New York, (1997), p. 387.
[56] Prentice, *op. cit.*, p. 146.

were controlled by the same small group of *elite*, who were all members of a close knit circle of men who were Tory in their politics and Anglican in their religion. Directly under the magistrates was the Deputy Chief Constable of Manchester, Joseph Nadin, who was hated by the majority of the working-class.[57] Archibald Prentice later described him as 'the real ruler of Manchester.'[58]

For a generation prior to Peterloo most of the new cotton manufacturers employed large numbers of immigrants from Ireland and Scotland who were either Dissenters or Roman Catholics. As a result of this, during the thirty years before Peterloo, Manchester was transformed from a predominantly Anglican into a largely Nonconformist town. In fact Nonconformists outnumbered Anglicans two to one both in Manchester and surrounding towns. The Unitarians in particular were most radical in their outlook. Thus: rivalry between the Establishment and Nonconformity was a prominent feature in the religious life of Manchester at the time of Peterloo.[59] This is reflected in the variety and number of Nonconformist chapels and churches, built during this period in and around Manchester that still stand today.

The Anglican attitude in Manchester on the question of Catholic Emancipation was one of even more 'uncompromising hostility.' For example, soon after Peterloo the Reverend Melville Horne, curate of St. Stephen's, Salford, denounced both the Radical Reformers and Roman Catholics in equal terms saying 'That the Radicals have publicly invited all Catholics to

[57] Read, *op. cit.*, p. 3.
[58] Archibald Prentice, *Historical Sketches and Personal Recollections of Manchester*, London, (1851), p. 34.
[59] Read, *op. cit.*, pp. 25-27.

join their banners is no novelty.' Earlier in May 1819 when a petition against Roman Catholic relief was prepared in Manchester, the local Anglican clergy were its biggest supporters.[60]

The Napoleonic Wars ended amidst riots which had been spasmodic for twenty-three years. For example, during the passing of the Corn Laws in 1815, the Houses of Parliament had to be defended by troops from menacing crowds.[61] In addition 300,000, disbanded soldiers suddenly swamped the already stretched employment market.[62] Aggravating the situation were those industries that had prospered during the war who like the iron industry found that the government no longer required their products.[63] There was also no need for new uniforms, blankets and other products to sustain the war effort which had thrown the cotton industry into deep depression.[64] 'The decline into wretchedness of large numbers of once-prosperous handloom weavers, the harsh conditions in the new mills and the terrible conditions of the industrial slums cast a dark shadow over the age.' [65]

By 1815, the ruling classes in Britain were still convinced that only they were fit to rule and their interests were those of society as a whole. Therefore, when Britain entered the economic crisis after the close of the Napoleonic War in 1815, the aristocratic rulers of Britain concentrated on protecting their own *property* and repressing all threats to their position of power

---

[60] *Ibid*, p. 27.
[61] Thompson, *op. cit.*, p. 660. *Working Class*
[62] Strong, *op. cit.*, p. 386.
[63] Hill, *op. cit.*, p. 69.
[64] Reid, *op. cit.*, p. 27.
[65] Aspin, *op. cit.*, p. 49.

and authority. There is no doubt that the Government and the ruling-classes still believed in the possibility of a popular revolution similar to the savage French Revolution that had taken place twenty years earlier. Their official reaction was to repress all agitation rather than deal with the causes of it.[66]

In 1815, at the end of the long endurance of war, there was fear, envy and greed, but little hope.[67] The reduction in the size of the navy added to the distress as the strength of the navy fell from 100,000 to 35,000 in 1816. Large numbers of labourers, on the verge of starvation, began spasmodic rioting, especially in the eastern counties.[68] In fact the four years following the end of the Napoleonic Wars in 1815 brought Britain closer to the brink of revolution than at any other time in her history.[69]

It should be noted that the return of peace in 1815 after the Napoleonic Wars and 23 years of conflict was not marked by a return to 'Church and King Deference' [70] but what was to become known as the 'heroic age of popular Radicalism.' [71] This was because the balance of popular sentiment had moved from Church and King to popular Radicalism which provided immunity to 'Church and King Propaganda' and the language of class conflict began to appear.[72] These were to be years of social unrest which found their voice in open-air meetings and the radical press. The radical voices that had been suppressed in the aftermath of the French Revolution and through the long endurance years of war, re-surfaced, especially, in the new

[66] Evans and Pledger, *op. cit.*, p. 8.
[67] J. H. Plumb, *England in The Eighteenth Century 1714-1815*, Harmondsworth, (1965), p. 214.
[68] Llewellyn Woodward, *The Age of Reform 1815-1870*, Oxford, (1962), p. 63.
[69] Strong, *op. cit.*, p. 386.
[70] Kidd, *op. cit.*, p. 89.
[71] Thompson, *op. cit.*, p. 660. *Working Class*
[72] John K. Walton *Lancashire A Social History 1558-1939*, Manchester, (1987), p. 153.

industrial areas of the country where reformer associations, called Hampden Clubs were established. These clubs were named after John Hampden, the man who had challenged the absolute rule of Charles I.[73]

In 1812 Major John Cartwright and Sir Francis Burdett had founded the Hampden Club in London. Cartwright then toured the country encouraging other parliamentary reformers to follow his example. His aim was to unite the middle-class moderates with radical members of the working-class. This frightened the authorities and led to his arrest in 1813 and 1815.[74] However, in 1816 a committee of the Hampden Club set to work upon a draft Reform Bill which it proposed to present to Parliament at the opening session of 1817. [75] By March 1817 there were forty clubs in the cotton districts of Lancashire, with about 8,000 members drawing much of their support from the smaller towns surrounding Manchester.[76] The Hampden Club founded in 1812 was by no means democratic in its constitution. Only landowners of substantial income were admitted to membership, and the object of the club was to stimulate a constitutional agitation for reform of the House of Commons on the lines laid down by the New Whig politicians who had founded the *Society of the Friends of the People* in 1792.[77]

The Hampden Clubs were eventually to be replaced by Political Unions who held open-air meetings and sent huge petitions to Parliament signed by thousands of people, only to find them ignored by Lord Liverpool's Government. For this

---

[73] Strong, *op. cit.*, p. 386.
[74] Reid, *op. cit.*, pp. 31-32.
[75] Davis, *op. cit.*, p. 7.
[76] Walton, *op. cit.*, p. 154.
[77] Davis, *op. cit.*, p. 6.

reason, the working-classes in the towns were demanding a reform of Parliament universal *male* suffrage, lower taxation, and relief from their poverty.[78]

With the end of the Napoleonic Wars in 1815, everybody had hoped for better times. However, the 'masked prosperity' of wartime ended, and the period between 1815 and 1830 proved to be one of deep depression.[79] The depression shook the nation at a time when poor living and working conditions, population growth, unemployment, and economic insecurity, had already created a state of discontent. These problems were aggravated by the fact that Lord Liverpool's Government's immediate reaction was to protect the interests of the wealthy-classes.[80] For example the commercial groups and the landed gentry put pressure on the Tory Government to abolish income tax. As it happens taxation was already crippling, due to the fact that the interest on the massive war debt still had to be paid. On 12th March 1816, Manchester local authorities presented a petition to the House of Commons against Property Tax. Although the Prime Minister William Pitt had introduced the Income Tax as an emergency measure during the war years, its selfish withdrawal led to a large increase in indirect taxation.[81]

The Government was forced to raise revenue by increasing sales tax on essential goods such as shoes, salt, tea, soap, paper, candles, tobacco, and even bricks. This meant for example a labourer earning £18 a year was forced to pay out half of his wages in the form of indirect taxation. Another major concern of the Government was to prevent agricultural depression. In an

---

[78] Strong, *op. cit.*, p. 386.
[79] Thomson, *op. cit.*, p. 285.
[80] Evans and Pledger, *op. cit.*, p.8.
[81] Thomson, *op. cit.*, p. 285.

effort to preserve the investments of wealthy landowners and to make England self-supporting in corn, the Corn Laws were passed to prevent foreign corn from being imported until the price of English corn reached 80s.0d. per quarter.[82] This forced the price of bread to a cost of about 1s. for a 2 lb. loaf, at a time when the usual wages of a labourer were 7s. a week. As a result for the next twenty years, the main subsistence of the working-classes was meal, potatoes and turnips, *bread* became a luxury.[83]

The Corn Law of 1815 highlighted the need for Parliamentary Reform and the working-classes led the way demanding radical reform, to enfranchise themselves. On the other hand the middle-classes and the Whigs took alarm and stood aloof, disapproving both of the Radical agitation and the Governments reprisals. Although the Whigs wanted to lead the middle-class they were divided on the Corn Laws because most of their leaders were nearly all from the landlord-class.[84]

There is also no doubt of course, that in 1816 the British people were still held down by force.[85] In spite of this it was largely in Lancashire where the Radical Reform Movement emerged. For example, as early as October 1816, there was an orderly open-air meeting in Blackburn. In January 1817, an Oldham meeting was preceded by a procession, complete with a band. The procession was headed by a Quaker apothecary to symbolize the peaceable intentions of the demonstrators.[86] In addition, the radicals carried on their propaganda by holding meetings, distributing pamphlets and the formation of clubs. As a result of this it was

---

[82] Evans and. Pledger, *op. cit.*, p. 8.
[83] Thomson, *op. cit.*, p. 285.
[84] George Macaulay Trevelyan, *British History in The Nineteenth Century 1782-1901*, London, (1925), p. 188.
[85] Thompson, *op. cit.*, p. 663.
[86] *Ibid*, p. 745.

not long 'before Lancashire men and women became the most, well informed and the most politically-conscious in the country.'[87]

Marlow highlights the fact that early radical activity had centred in London. This was largely because from the Glorious Revolution of 1688, the people had been given the right to petition the reigning monarch about their grievances. Although at this time the Prince Regent was standing in for King George III, who in 1811 had lost his mind so that petitions were presented to the Prince Regent instead. Another way the radicals aired their grievances in London was by calling for a mass-meeting. After the petition had been adopted, the crowds usually dispersed peacefully.[88]

Henry Hunt travelled to London to extend his reputation as an open-air orator and gained much popularity by declaring for manhood suffrage. This was a proposal which Cartwright had abandoned in deference to Burdett and other moderate members of the Hampden Club.[89] On 2nd December 1816, Hunt was the main speaker at a large popular meeting held in the Spa Fields, London.[90] At this time of course, the main interest of the working class in demanding political reform was to gain representatives in Parliament who could legislate on their behalf to put an end to their poverty.[91] In fact it was Henry Hunt who 'inaugurated the radical mass platform to put pressure on the central government for constitutional reform, to include universal manhood suffrage, annual parliaments and the ballot

---

[87] Aspin, *op. cit.*, p. 49.
[88] Marlow, *op. cit.*, p. 56. *Peterloo Massacre*
[89] Davis, *op. cit.*, p. 7.
[90] Dinwiddy, *op. cit.*, p. 25.
[91] Evans and Pledger, *op. cit.*, p. 8.

for all. There is no doubt that this offended some members of the reform movement and middle-class reformers who favoured direct-taxation, universal suffrage and close co-operation with the Whig opposition.' [92] After the Spa Fields meeting there was some rioting and many demonstrators were arrested.

Following the Spa Fields riots Lord Liverpool's Government introduced the Gagging Acts in 1816, forbidding public meetings except under licence from the magistrates. Later in the year a stone was thrown through the window of the Prince Regents coach. The following year also witnessed the Derbyshire Insurrection, a pathetic outbreak of unemployed framework knitters, deliberately set up by one of the Governments most active secret agents Oliver the Spy, an *agent provocateur*. Following a trial three men were convicted and hanged while eleven other men were transported to Australia for life as convicts.[93]

There were a number of Radical Reform meetings in Manchester throughout 1816 and 1817, for example on November 4th 1816, John Knight addressed about 5,000 people assembled in St Peter's Field to 'take into consideration the present distressed state of the country.' This first reform meeting in St Peter's Field caused considerable alarm to the authorities and in the next January a meeting of the inhabitants was held to consider 'the necessity of adopting additional measures for the maintenance of peace.' [94]

The Blanketeers plan was first announced at an open-air meeting held in Manchester on 3rd March 1817. The purpose of

---

[92] Belchem, *op. cit.*, p. 9.
[93] Hill, *op. cit.*, p. 68.
[94] Thomson, *op. cit.*, p. 285.

the meeting was to petition against the *Suspension of the Habeas Corpus Act*, which was to receive the royal assent on the following day.[95]Another meeting followed on 10th March 1817, when 12,000 people gathered in St Peter's Field to support the march of the Blanketeers. This meeting had been largely organised by John Bagguley, Samuel Drummond and John Johnston.[96] A number of those assembled decided to march *en masse* to London in order to personally present to the Prince Regent a petition for the redress of their grievances. It has been described as the first hunger march in British history. They were protesting about the government's economic policies and in particular the Corn Laws which had driven up the price of *bread*. Each man carried a blanket in preparation for the journey. Those who took part in the march were nicknamed the *Blanketeers*. However, this action turned out to be ill-advised, and ended with disastrous consequences for the men who took part.[97]

The machinery of repression was already in motion however,[98] and the Manchester magistrates called out the Kings Dragoon Guards to disperse the meeting.[99] Then, fearing a mass demonstration in London the Manchester, authorities sent the soldiers in pursuit of the Marchers.[100] The Reverend Mr Hay's account of the Blanketeers meeting of 10th March 1817 to the Home Secretary appears in an extract in (H. O. 40. 5, *Manchester Papers*, No. 11.). He explains that the magistrates

---

[95] Davis, *op. cit.*, p. 14.

[96] Read, *op. cit.*, p. 39.

[97] T. Swindles, *Manchester Streets and Manchester Men*, Manchester, (1908), p. 164. ; for the *Petition of the Blanketeers to the Prince Regent* see *Hay Scrap Book*, Vol. VII, Chetham Library, Manchester, p. 161.

[98] Walton, *op. cit.*, p. 154.

[99] Arthur Redford, *The History of Local Government in Manchester*, London, (1939), p. 248.

[100] Swindles, *op. cit.*, p. 164.

had conferred with Major-General Sir John Byng on the previous day and had agreed upon the course of action. He writes:

At an early hour this morning large parties were seen flocking to St. Peter's Church-the place of the meeting-and soon afterwards a very large concourse of people as I have estimated about 12,000 had assembled. Some very numerous parties marched two abreast regularly and many others with knapsacks bags and &c. The ground was occupied much earlier than usual, and about a quarter before ten the orators began to harangue the mob from the cart...After a certain time part of the mob was observed to move off in a regular march, those who had knapsacks and bags amongst them...It was ascertained who the orators were, and that Bagguley & Drummond were two of them. Agst. These warrants had been issued by the Magistrates here, and a further warrant from your Lordship had just arrived. Notice being given to the Magistrates that the parties who were to seize these two men were ready, we all proceeded to the ground & had the satisfaction of seeing these two men taken as well as one Williams who acted as Secretary. This was effected by a very ready and neat movement of the military. The Cart whence the orators harangued was-taken the owner of the Cart is in custody. Mr H. Watson both before and after this requested the populace to disperse –but with no visible effect. The ground was now kept by a party of the King's Dragoon Guards under Col. Teesdale-about 20 other persons were taken, [arrested] It was soon determined that a party of the Military accompanied by 2 Magistrates, Mr. H. Watson & Mr Ethelston shd. Follow the mob who had marched, as I have described towards Stockport on their way to London...it was overtaken on the Lancashire side of the river, just before wd. have got into Stockport & that 215 were taken. They were brought back under two escorts. The 1st party of prisoners consisted of 48; the latter of 167. Short examinations were taken of the first party the second did not arrive until too late. The proceedings will go on as fast as may be & the result communicated to Your Lordship.[101]

Yet in spite of this 200 Blanketeers arrived at Macclesfield, 50 got as far as Leek, 20 reached Ashbourne, and a few reached Derby.[102] In fact one man, Abel Couldwell, of Stalybridge, actually reached London and managed to present his petition to Lord Sidmouth to be delivered to the Prince Regent.[103]

Shortly after the Blanketeers meeting the magistrates and the local authorities were formally thanked by Lord Liverpool's Government for their decisive action in dispersing the meeting and arresting offenders. [104] Michael Kennedy in his *Portrait of Manchester* (1970) suggests that only 'some of the leaders were arrested and some of the marchers went as far as Macclesfield before their disorganised action fizzled out in failure.' [105] When in fact over two hundred men were arrested and thrown into the

---

[101] Davis, *op. cit.*, p. 32.; H.O. 40. 5, *Manchester Papers*, No. 11.
[102] Swindles *op. cit.*, p. 164.
[103] Pauline Gregg, *A Social And Economic History Of Britain 1760-1972*, London, (1973), p. 90.
[104] *Manchester Mercury*, 25th March 1817.
[105] Michael Kennedy, *Portrait of Manchester*, (The Portrait Series), London, (1970), p. 64.

New Bailey Prison [now Strangeways] for taking part in the March of the Blanketeers. Five men regarded as ringleaders were sent to London under warrants from the Home Secretary. Nine other men were sent to Lancaster to be tried on the charge of 'tumultuous petitioning,' but were released after five months imprisonment as it was doubtful that a jury would convict them. Twenty-one other marchers were committed to Chester Gaol, although fifteen of these men were released after they had taken the 'oath of allegiance.' John Bagguley, John Johnson, Samuel Drummond and John Knight, were committed by the Privy Council to various county gaols.[106]

The ill-treatment and wholesale arrests of these *Blanketeers* had created indignation, and leading Manchester Radicals met in a secret committee to discuss what should be done. This came to be known as the Ardwick Conspiracy. However, after receiving information from government spies the local authorities were convinced that an insurrection would begin on 30th March.[107] Samuel Bamford and seven others were arrested for complicity in the Ardwick scheme and were taken to London. However, the Home Office complained 'that they had been arrested for high treason without any depositions having first been given against them' and later they discharged the men concerned.[108]

In 1817, Lord Liverpool's Government feared revolution and suspended the *Habeas Corpeas Act*.[109] The Act made it illegal to keep a man in prison without trial and its suspension meant that men suspected of being agitators or revolutionaries could be

---

[106] Davis, *op. cit.*, p. 16.
[107] Turner, *op. cit.*, p. 257.
[108] Davis, *op. cit.*, p. 19.
[109] Stamp, A.H., *A Social and Economic History of England From 1700 to 1970*, London, (1979), p. 133.

imprisoned for as long as the government wished.[110] 'The local authorities in Manchester reflected the government anxiety.'[111] Later in 1817, the Manchester authorities announced that they had received information of 'a most daring and traitorous conspiracy the subject of which is nothing less than open Insurrection and Rebellion.' This hysterical outburst led to the formation of the *Manchester Yeomanry Cavalry*, a volunteer force of which more was to be heard in August 1819.[112] On 21st June 1817, *The Manchester Chronicle* reported:

> A meeting at the Manchester Police Office on June 19th decided under the present circumstances a force of yeomanry cavalry should be embodied.[113]

In fact the Manchester and Salford Yeomanry had been formed in 1817 to deal with the 'Radical Danger' in particular. [114]

Another aspect of Lord Sidmouth's policy was the employment of paid spies who often also acted as *agents provocateurs.* The Home Office had a special fund which it distributed to magistrates to maintain their spies. Very often the Home Office was approached by volunteers who were anxious to be employed as spies or informers. These people included soldiers, labourers, convicts and members of the general public.[115] Records show that the Manchester magistrates used this fund freely. After the great success in which Yorkshire Luddites had

---

[110] Evans and Pledger, *op. cit.*, p. 8.
[111] Kidd, *op. cit.*, p. 90.
[112] Thomson, *op. cit.*, p. 287.
[113] *The Manchester Chronicle* 21st June 1817.
[114] Read, *op. cit.*, p. 81.
[115] Darvall, *op. cit.*, pp. 274-275.

been arrested in 1812 and convicted on the evidence of spies, it was now being used in Manchester.[116] The Reverend Mr Hay supplied cash to Deputy Chief Constable Nadin to operate his own web of spies. As early as 1817 when John Bagguley and Samuel Drummond were organising workers meetings they were always on the lookout for Nadin's spies.[117] During the great strike of 1818, according to a government spy: 'The spinners marched by Piccadilly on Tuesday and was 23½ minets in going by.' [118]

Throughout the time frame of these years Government spies including the notorious Oliver the Spy were busily stirring up starving operatives to sedition. However, Oliver went too far while trying to implicate some middle-class reformers in Lancashire and the spy business which had long been carried out with impunity among the working-classes was promptly exposed in Parliament by the Whig opposition.[119]

Although the Hampden Clubs did not survive 1817 the radical campaign was kept alive through similarly organised Union Societies. The first was founded in Stockport in October 1818, which was largely the work of the Reverend Joseph Harrison, with the unusual title of the *Stockport Union for the Promotion of Human Happiness.*[120] Moreover the Union Societies spread through the cotton districts as rapidly as the Hampden Clubs during the renewed economic depression of 1819.[121] By August 1819 all of Manchester's surrounding towns had at least one

---

[116] Reid, *op. cit.*, p. 25.
[117] *Ibid*, p. 45.
[118] Thompson, *op. cit.*, p. 747.
[119] Trevelyan, *op. cit.*, pp. 188-189.
[120] Read, *op. cit.*, p. 47.
[121] Walton, *op. cit.*, p. 154.

Union Society who sent contingents to Peterloo. Women's Union Societies were also established who also founded Radical Sunday Schools to attract pupils away from loyalist schools.[122]

The Union Societies were supported by the Radical Press. By 1819 the Radical Reform Movement spread throughout the country through three main channels namely, Union Societies, mass meetings and through the Radical Press.[123] In the absence of a national organisation, local societies took their lead from the Radical Press. Between 1816 and 1820 Radical propaganda found its voice in the hand-press and the weekly periodicals. T. J. Wooler, the editor of *Black Dwarf,* commanded the largest Radical audience at this time. Radicals who preferred a newspaper could read the *Manchester Observer* whose circulation approached that of the *Black Dwarf* by the end of 1819.[124] However, a wave of prosecutions against the Radical Press resulted in some heavy sentences and some triumphant acquittals as in the cases of Hone and the *Black Dwarf* newspaper.[125]

Between 1817 and 1819, the works of Cobbett and Hone were extensively read by the working-classes, and in many districts reading groups were formed for the purpose of hearing them read. At the time readers were scarce and Radicals like Elijah Ridings in Manchester were selected to act as reader for the groups to which they belonged.[126] There is no doubt that periodicals like Cobbett's *Political Register* and the *Black Dwarf* played a big part in co-ordinating the Reform

[122] Kidd, *op. cit.*, p. 91.
[123] Read, *op. cit.*, p. 46.
[124] Thompson, *op. cit.*, pp. 739-42.
[125] Tevelyan, *op.cit.*, p. 189.
[126] Swindles, *op. cit.*, p. 187.

Movement.[127] In addition the 'caricaturists in the Radical Press mercilessly ridiculed and criticised what they believed to be an extravagant and corrupt ruling-class headed by the decadent Prince Regent the future George IV.'[128] Thomas Wooler however, the editor of *The Black Dwarf*, found himself in gaol for most of the time for inciting the public to overthrow the government.[129] At the end of 1819 at the height of Hone and Cruikshank's brilliant lampoons *The Political House that Jack Built* was reported to have sold over 100,000 copies.[130]

Both Hone and Wooler were on bail, awaiting trial for 'sedition' and 'blasphemy' when on the 9th June the Spa Fields prisoners faced trial at the Old Bailey for High Treason. On the other hand when the *Habeas Corpus Act* was suspended, William Cobbett, suspecting quite rightly perhaps, that he was in the firing line migrated to America. William Hone immediately stepped in to Cobbett's place and published his own *Reformists Register*. [131] In 1819 a number of new periodicals appeared in London. These included the *Medusa*, the *Democratic Recorder* the *Cap of Liberty*, and the *Republican*, each displaying their own aggressive style. However, except for the *Republican* none of these periodicals lasted more than several months.[132]

In 1819, following wave of economic distress Reform agitation flared up again. Since *Habeas Corpeas* was no longer suspended monster meetings of the working-classes were held in the industrial districts to demand universal suffrage.[133] On 18th

---

[127] Dinwiddy, *op. cit.*, p. 37.
[128] Strong, *op. cit.*, p. 386.
[129] Schama, *op. cit.*, p. 132.
[130] Thompson, *op. cit.*, p. 743.
[131] Jackson, *op. cit.*, 76-77.
[132] Dinwiddy, *op. cit.*, p. 37.
[133] Trevelyan, *op. cit.*, p. 189.

January 1819 Henry Hunt presided over a meeting of 8,000 workers on St Peter's Field which unanimously voted against petitioning to be replaced by a Remonstrance instead. Another meeting was held on St Peter's Field on 21st June 1819. This meeting was called for by the distressed weavers to petition either for relief for their distresses or for assisted emigration to North America. However, the weavers were dissuaded from petitioning for assisted emigration as the answer to their problems. Instead the Radicals Saxton and Walker convinced them that the Radical Reform Movement was their answer.[134]

Working-class radicalism drew most of its support from the industrial areas of Manchester and all the surrounding districts and had a massive following, due to the hard times. Although some of this support came from the union societies, most of it came from the thousands of handloom weavers, 'whose fervour and fanaticism gave to Manchester radicalism an intensity which was unrivalled throughout the land.' A correspondent wrote to a Manchester newspaper in 1819 who declared: 'A radical complete constitutional reform, we want nothing but this…to mend our markets and give every poor man plenty of work and good wages for doing it.' [135]

In fact there were a number of mass open-air meetings in most large towns throughout June and July 1819. Lord Liverpool's Government, local authorities and even middle-class reformers were alarmed at the proliferation and character of these demonstrations, fuelled by government informants and spies who maintained that 'insurrectionary plotting lay behind them.'

---

[134] Read, *op. cit.*, pp. 106-109.
[135] Malcolm Bee, *Industrial Revolution and Social Reform in the Manchester Region, Manchester*, (1997), p. 11.

This explains why by 1819, Manchester and the surrounding districts were practically under military occupation.[136]

By way of explanation, Manchester's 'loyalists' in 1819 were those who actually supported the action of the authorities at Peterloo. They were divided into two groups, the High Tory on the one hand and the Pittites on the other. The High Tories wanted to maintain the *status quo* in church and state. Whilst the Pittites were mostly cotton manufactures who wanted commercial reform in the form of greater freedom for trade and limited reform of Parliament to give Manchester some commercial representation at Westminster. The High Tories were almost all Anglicans and either magistrates or clergy. 'It was this group that included many of the men responsible for the Peterloo Massacre.'[137] There is no doubt that the 'loyalists' in Manchester associated the Radical Reform Movement with revolution.[138] On the other hand the Tory magistrates, yeomanry, constables, and radical leaders were usually identified with the social classes they represented.[139]

During the summer of 1819 there occurred a mass mobilization of popular support for political reform.[140] This was reflected by the fact that the weeks leading up to Peterloo witnessed lots of small meetings followed by more impressive demonstrations in regional centres like Manchester in June, and in Birmingham, Leeds and London in July.[141] In addition there had been a number of reform meetings held in various parts of Lancashire

---

[136]Thomson, *op. cit.*, p. 285.

[137] Read, *op. cit.*, p. 74.

[138] Kirk, *op. cit.*, p. 61.

[139] Diana Donald, 'The Power of Print: Graphic Images of Peterloo,' *Manchester Regional History Review*, Vol. iii, (1989), p. 21.

[140] *Ibid*, p. 61.

[141] Thompson, *op. cit.*, p. 749.

over the previous two months. These meetings took place at Oldham, Ashton and Stockport in June, followed by Blackburn, Rochdale, Macclesfield, in July, and Leigh in early August. These meetings were a clear demonstration of the extent of popular support which the Radical Reform Movement enjoyed. It also showed how well the movement was organised, with Reform Unions drawing massive crowds much to the alarm of the Manchester authorities.[142]

---

[142] Bush, *op. cit.*, p. 38.

Orator Henry Hunt
Manchester Library and Information Service:
Manchester Archives and Local Studies.

Orator Henry Hunt had come forward as a champion of the people's rights.[143] Although he came from a privileged background he had earned the reputation as being the best public speaker in England. He was also the most popular radical leader in Lancashire, drawing large crowds. It was reported that during 1819, Hunt was welcomed in a Lancashire village with the road carpeted with flowers.[144] Records of songs that were sung in Lancashire and around Manchester in particular included this single verse:

> With Henry Hunt we'll go, we'll go,
> With Henry Hunt we'll go;
> We'll raise the cap of liberty,
> In spite of Nadin Joe.[145]

At a Radical Sunday School in Manchester it was reported that the 'monitors wore locket-portraits of Henry Hunt around their necks.' [146]
As it happens, unlike the working-class Radicals, the middle-class reformers in Manchester by 1819 controlled no extensive network of agitation. They remained no more than a group of like-minded friends 'a small but determined band'[147] and disliked Hunt, 'dismissing him as a vain publicity seeker.'[148] In fact the middle-class reformers seem to have been completely cut off from the working-class reformers. For example John

---

[143] Prentice, *op. cit.*, p. 146.
[144] Thompson, *op. cit.*, p. 689.
[145] John Harland, *Ballads and Songs of Lancashire*, (second edition), London, (1875), p. 195.
[146] Read, *op. cit.*, p. 54. *Manchester Observer*, 29th January, 1819.
[147] *Ibid*, p. 57.
[148] Turner, *British Politics in the Age of Reform, Manchester*, (1999), p. 116.

Knight a small manufacturer was the secretary of the Manchester Constitutional Society but he was the only representative of that class in the Society. Furthermore Knight was unable to induce any of the gentlemen or any of the respectable-reformers to take the chair at the inaugural meeting.[149] Throughout 1819, the Tory newspapers criticised the Radical Reform meetings that had been held during the year. Furthermore, the Tories got together and on the 9th July at a police office meeting formed a new Special Committee of Magistrates to strengthen the civil power, suggesting the swearing in of extra special constables. This was soon followed by advertisements appearing in newspapers calling for volunteers to join the local yeomanry.[150]

The Radical *Manchester Observer* claimed to have a circulation of 4000 by the middle of 1819, with a readership of several times that number.[151] Hunt believed that the *Manchester Observer* was 'the only newspaper in England...fairly and honestly devoted to such a reform as would give the people their whole rights.' [152] In more recent years David Ayerst in his book *Guardian Biography of a Newspaper* describes the Radical newspaper as the 'extremist *Manchester Observer*.' [153] However, although the *Manchester Observer* continued its coverage of reform meetings in support of the radical cause, by the end of 1819 its owners faced indictments for libel and fines for failure to pay stamp duties. There seems little doubt that the Radical Reformers on the one hand and the Loyalists on the

[149] Davis, *op. cit.*, p. 4.
[150] Turner, *op. cit.*, p. 117. *British politics in an age of reform*
[151] Walton, *op. cit.*, p. 155. *Manchester Observer*, 28th August, 1819.
[152] Read, *op. cit.*, pp. 55-56. *Manchester Observer*, 14th August, 1819.
[153] David Ayerst, *Guardian Biography of a Newspaper*, London, (1971), p. 18.

other expected some form of confrontation to tip the balance in their favour.[154] Therefore it is not surprising that the animosity between them was becoming very intense.[155]

The policy in Regency England was to call on the regular army in troubled times to act as a police force [156] but the main representatives of law and order were the local magistrates, many of whom, like the Manchester magistrates, belonged to an elite oligarchy having little sympathy with the working-class or even with the new smaller mill owners. Their main anxiety was that there would be an assault on property by the mob. Because there was no organised police force, they often swore-in Special Constables or asked to the Home Secretary Lord Sidmouth to authorise the use of the army.[157]

The local authorities responsible for maintaining law and order in Regency England had four organisations to call on. These were the police, voluntary defence associations, yeomanry or militia and the regular armed forces. However, the police were almost non-existent. The regular professional police force of modern times was introduced during the next decade. Therefore lacking a force of regular paid constables the towns and villages had to depend upon special constables, either paid or unpaid. Whenever danger threatened one of the first steps the authorities took was to enrol a force of unpaid Special Constables. These men were sworn in as Special Constables and peace officers and given authority to disperse mobs and arrest offenders upon a magistrates warrant. Large numbers of these constables, mostly

---

[154] Turner, *op. cit.*, p. 262.
[155] Turner, *op. cit.*, p. 117. *British politics in an age of reform*
[156] White, *op. cit.*, p. 190-91.
[157] Asa Briggs, *The Age of Improvement 1783-1876*, London, (1979), p. 213.

unpaid, were enrolled during Regency England disturbances.[158] There is no doubt that this was the policy adopted by the Manchester authorities before the Radical Reform meeting held on 16th August 1819. In fact preparations by the Manchester authorities were very similar to those made the day before the Blanketeers meeting held in St Peter's Field in 1817. [159]

As we have seen by 1819, deference had been considerably weakened in whole regions of England by Dissent, Methodism and also challenged by Luddism, the Hampden Clubs and the Union Societies.[160] In addition Radical activity in Lancashire in 1819 was particularly strong. This was due to a Radical Press, Radical mass meetings, Radical Schools and Societies, and of course the Radical Programme itself. This largely explains although it does not justify the fear and panic of the local authorities at Peterloo. On the one hand the Manchester magistrates were more concerned with what was happening in Lancashire, whilst on the other Lord Sidmouth and the government at Westminster could see a pattern of Radical activity emerging throughout the country. Therefore by 1819 the Radical background to Peterloo can only be described as being nation-wide.[161]

To conclude, the background to Peterloo lay in the social and political discontent which helped create the Radical Reform Movement in Britain during the late 18th and 19th centuries. With the ending of the Napoleonic War in 1815, when Napoleon was defeated at the Battle of Waterloo, 300,000 soldiers and sailors were disbanded and returned home. This along with

---

[158] Darvall, *op. cit.*, pp. 250-252.
[159] Davis, *op. cit.*, p. 32.
[160] Thompson, *op. cit.*, p. 737.
[161] Read, *op. cit.*, p. 56.

unprecedented population growth, high food prices created by the Corn Laws, along with mass unemployment, social and political unrest became widespread. The existing out dated system of parliamentary representation meant that many of the urban centres that had grown rapidly in the Industrial Revolution, like Manchester and the surrounding towns, had no Member of Parliament to look after their interests.[162]

It was against this background that the mood was set for the August meeting which was the climax of a series of political meetings held in Manchester, and its satellite towns in 1819, a year of industrial depression and high food prices. The organisers intended that a mass-meeting would be a great peaceful demonstration of discontent and its political purpose was to put pressure on the Central Government to bring about Parliamentary Reform.[163] However, working-class demands for political and economic reform were more often than not met with brutal government action.[164]

---

[162] Dorothy Marshall, *Industrial England 1776-1851*, London, (1982), p. 136.

[163] Kidd, *op. cit.*, p. 87.

[164] Marshall, *op. cit.*, p. 136

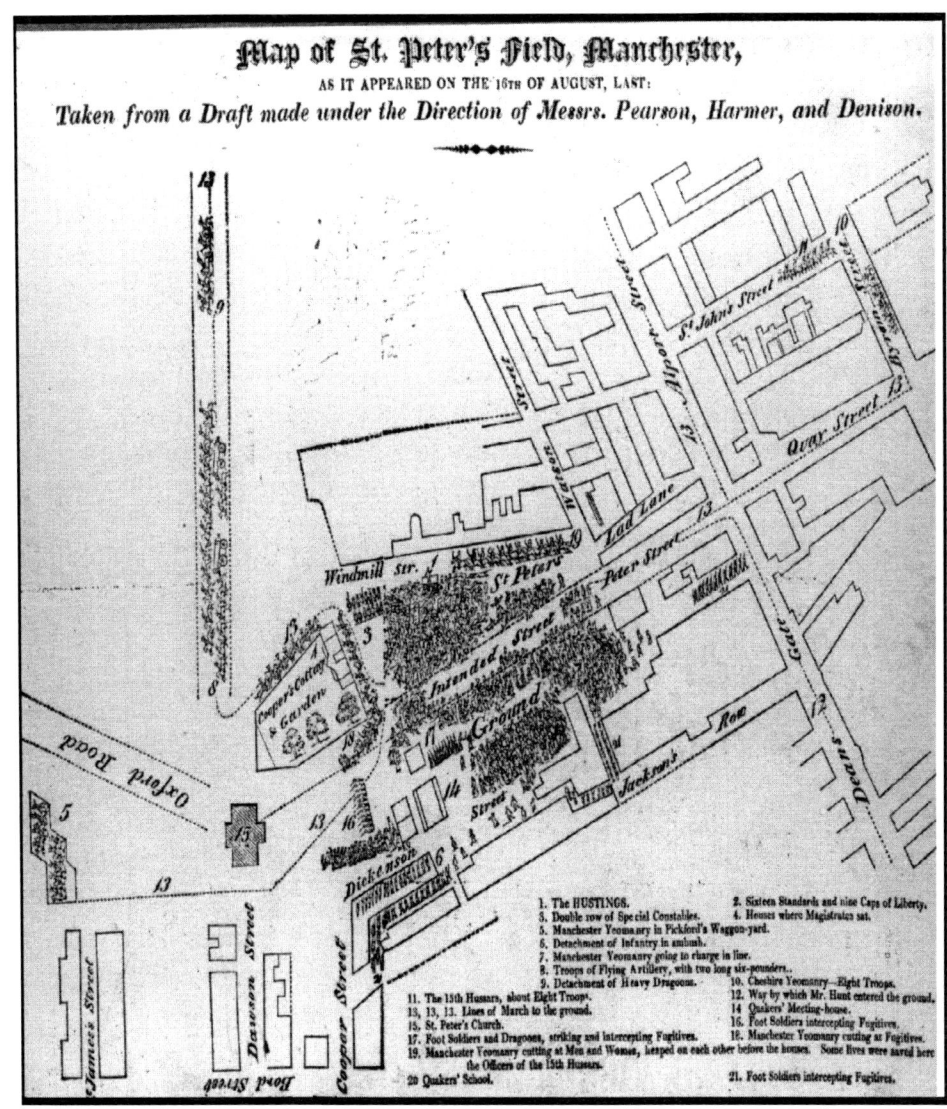

Map of St. Peter's Field, Manchester,

AS IT APPEARED ON THE 16TH OF AUGUST, LAST:

Taken from a Draft made under the Direction of Messrs. Pearson, Harmer, and Denison.

1. The HUSTINGS.
2. Sixteen Standards and nine Caps of Liberty.
3. Double row of Special Constables.
4. Houses where Magistrates sat.
5. Manchester Yeomanry in Pickford's Waggon-yard.
6. Detachment of Infantry in ambush.
7. Manchester Yeomanry going to charge in line.
8. Troops of Flying Artillery, with two long six-pounders.
9. Detachment of Heavy Dragoons.
10. Cheshire Yeomanry—Eight Troops.
11. The 15th Hussars, about Eight Troops.
12. Way by which Mr. Hunt entered the ground.
13, 13, 13. Lines of March to the ground.
14 Quakers' Meeting-house.
15. St. Peter's Church.
16. Foot Soldiers intercepting Fugitives.
17. Foot Soldiers and Dragoons, striking and intercepting Fugitives.
18. Manchester Yeomanry cutting at Fugitives.
19. Manchester Yeomanry cutting at Men and Women, heaped on each other before the houses. Some lives were saved here by the Officers of the 15th Hussars.
20 Quakers' School.
21. Foot Soldiers intercepting Fugitives.

Manchester Library and Information Service: Manchester Archives and Local Studies

53

Chapter Two

Peterloo Massacre

There can be no doubt that the condemnation of William Hulton and the Special Select Committee of Magistrates is justified. Nobody can deny what the mass meeting was all about. The radical protesters were carrying banners demanding-Universal Suffrage, No Boroughmongering, and No Corn Laws. Hulton and the Regency Tories refused the masses their political rights, and also expected many of them to acquiesce in near starvation caused by the deep post-war economic depression.[165]

The major myths surrounding Peterloo or the Peterloo Massacre can be identified as follows: firstly, there had been no premeditation by the Select Committee of Magistrates to disperse the meeting by force and that the magistrates were only guilty of incompetence or ill-judgement and that everything happened by chance.[166] Secondly, most of the injuries were caused by the fleeing crowd. Thirdly, the 15th Hussars only used the flats of their swords.[167] Fourthly, only 11 people were killed and only 400 people were injured.[168] An additional misconception in the historiography is that the Irish population of Manchester did not become integrated with the movement for Parliamentary Reform.[169] It will be argued that other

[165] Donald Read, Review of 'Peteterloo: The Case Reopened by Robert Warmsley,' *History*, Vol., 55, (1970), pp. 138-140.
[166] J. Stevenson, *Popular Disturbances in England 1700-1870*, London, (1979), p. 284.
[167] Kidd, *op. cit.*, p. 94.
[168] Read, *op. cit.*, p. 140.
[169] Thompson, *op. cit.*, pp. 707-708.

interpretations of these issues, based on the evidence available clearly show that such myths should not be believed.

Plans to hold the meeting in St Peter's Field began early in July and the following official announcement appeared in the *Manchester Observer* on 31st July:

> The public are respectfully informed, that a MEETING will be held here on Monday the 9th August 1819 on the Area near St. PETER'S CHURCH, to take into consideration, the most speedy and effectual mode of obtaining Radical Reform in the Commons House of Parliament; being fully convinced, that nothing less can remove the intolerable evils under which the People of this Country have so long, and do still, groan: and also to consider the propriety of the 'Unrepresented Inhabitants of Manchester' electing a Person to represent them in Parliament; and the adopting Major Cartwright's Bill.
>
> H. HUNT, Esq. In the Chair.[170]

However, after the magistrates were informed that the meeting would include the election of a 'representative to Parliament' they declared the meeting to be illegal and on the same day the 31st July, the magistrates in Manchester published their response assuming that it would be in accordance with Home Office advice, which read as follows:

---

[170] *Manchester Observer*, 31st July, 1819.

Whereas it appears by an advertisement in the Manchester Observer paper of this day, that a PUBLIC AND ILLEGAL MEETING is convened for Monday, the 9th day of August next, to be held on the AREA NEAR SAINT PETER'S CHURCH in Manchester. We, the undersigned Magistrates, acting for the Counties Palatine of Lancaster and Chester, do hereby caution all Persons to abstain AT THEIR PERIL from attending such ILLEGAL MEETING.[171]

Consequently the organisers postponed the meeting. However by the 6th August the Radicals had amended their notice which was accompanied by hundreds of signatures and the following notice appeared in the *Manchester Observer*:

A requisition having been presented to the Borough-reeve and Constables of Manchester, signed by above 700 inhabitants, requesting them to call a public meeting 'to consider the propriety of adopting the most LEGAL AND EFFECTUAL means of obtaining a REFORM in the Commons Houses of Parliament,' and they having declined to call such a meeting, therefore the under-signed Requisitions give NOTICE that a public meeting will be held, on the area, near St Peter's Church, for the above mentioned purpose on Monday the 16th instant. The Chair to be taken by H. Hunt Esq, at 12 o'clock.[172]

---

[171] Marlow, *op. cit.*, p. 103. *Peterloo Massacre*
[172] *Manchester Observer*, 7th August, 1819.

In fact the magistrates had no power to prohibit meetings for such a lawful purpose, and therefore kept silent. Therefore the reformers interpreted this as a tacit permission to proceed, and announced that the meeting would be held in St Peter's Field on the 16th August.[173] However as Read points out 'by allowing the people to assemble the magistrates gave them the impression that they accepted the meeting as legal and that they would not interfere.' [174] Nevertheless although the magistrates had no power to prohibit the meeting beforehand, they assumed that it would turn out to be illegal, and made plans to disperse it by the use of civil and military force.[175]

In the descriptive words of Joyce Marlow 'from first light, thousands of men women and children walked in from villages and hamlets clad in their best clothes, shabby as those were, clutching their packets of food. The majority were aware of the seriousness of the meeting and the tensions that existed, the occasion was regarded as a day out, a few hours away from the handloom or mill or the miseries of their existence.' [176]

On the 16th August 1819 the *Manchester Observer* reported that the morning was extremely fine and 'well calculated to produce the attendance of an immense assemblage.'[177]As expected throughout the morning contingents of radical Reformers marched in an orderly formation to music played by local amateur bands. They came from Bolton, Bury, Chadderton, Cheadle, Failsworth, Middleton, Newton Heath, Miles Platting,

---

[173] Redford, *op.cit.,* p. 252.
[174] Read, *op. cit.*, p. 122.
[175] Redford, *op. cit.*, p. 252.
[176] Joyce Marlow, 'The Day of Peterloo,' *Manchester Regional History Review*, Vol. iii, (1989), p. 3.
[177] *Manchester Observer*, 16th August, 1819.

Oldham, and Rochdale, Royton, Saddleworth, Stockport and other surrounding towns.[178]

In the early hours of the 16th August the bill-posting men were out in force in the streets of Manchester, pasting notices on every spare wall and notice board:

> The Borough Reeves and the Constables of Manchester and Salford most earnestly recommend the peaceable and well disposed inhabitants of the two towns, as much as possible, to remain in their own houses, during the whole of this day, Monday, August 16th inst., and to keep their children and servants within doors.[179]

The author's maternal Great, Great, Great grandfather Elijah Ridings who was a radical poet in the post–Napoleonic era took an active part in the Reform Movement, and at the age of 17 years led the Newton Heath and Miles Platting contingents to the Peterloo Meeting in 1819.[180] Most families that are long-term residents of Manchester and the surrounding towns can almost certainly guarantee that some of their ancestors were there too.

All reports agree that reformers were waving flags and many were carrying banners inscribed with statements like *Vote by Ballot*, *Annual Parliaments*, *Universal Suffrage*, *No Boroughmongering*, and *No Corn Laws*. The Lees and Saddleworth Union contingent led by Dr. Healy carried a black banner with the words in white letters, *Equal Representation or*

---

[178] S. Bamford, *Passages in the Life of a Radical*, I, Manchester, (1844), pp. 198-200.
[179] Warmsley, *op. cit.*, p. 147.
[180] L. M. Angus Butterworth, *Lancashire Literary Worthies*, St Andrews, (1980), p 123. ; Swindles, *op. cit.*, p. 187. *Manchester Guardian*, 19th October, 1872.

Death; this was also accompanied by a heart and two clasped hands with *Love*, inscribed on it. This disturbed the Manchester authorities and it was largely because of this that Dr. Healy was arrested after the meeting.[181] Some of the radical contingents were led by ex-soldiers who had fought at Waterloo. These men acted as drill masters, and there is no doubt that the reformers were proud of them. However, they marched at the front of their contingents not as 'paramilitaries but as patriots.'[182]

There were also large numbers of working-class women in all-female contingents, dressed in white and with their own women leaders and carrying their own flags.[183] The vicious portrayal of women in the cartoons and press reports of the time deliberately denies women their femininity as they are seen as a dual threat not only to the aristocracy's dominance over society but also of male dominance over women. Thus: in the eyes of the authorities if female reformers wanted to behave like men they would be treated with equal ferocity with no gallantry shown in order to teach them an unforgettable lesson.[184]

The 180th anniversary of Peterloo witnessed an essay by Tom Waghorn in his article the *Killing Field* appearing in *The Making of Manchester*, (1999), in which he says:

> Many of the weavers had marched from Oldham and Middleton over bare moorland, or across the fields from Stockport. They had arrived at Peter's Field in dignified

---

[181] R. J. White, *Waterloo to Peterloo*, London, (1957), p. 190.

[182] Robert Poole, 'The March to Peterloo: Politics and Festivity in Late Georgian England,' *Past and Present*, No 192, August, (2006), p. 148.

[183] Michael Bush, 'The Women at Peterloo : The Impact of Female Reform on the Manchester Meeting of 16 August 1819,' *History*, Vol. 89, No. 293. January (2004), pp. 209-210.

[184] Bush, *op. cit.*, p. 2. *Casualties of Peterloo*

cohorts, preceded by bands and banners, and complaining about the appalling conditions in mills and cottages....Mancunians were puzzled by the action of magistrate William Hulton, who ordered the dispersal of the meeting. He had the reputation of being a sincere and conscientious man, and townsfolk said he made a disastrous mistake in a moment of blind panic.[185]

Tom Waghorn's description is not really a true picture and in contrast I agree with Donald Read who says:

There can be no doubt that the condemnation of William Hulton and the Special Select Committee of Magistrates is justified. Nobody can deny what the mass meeting was all about. The radical protesters were carrying banners demanding-Universal Suffrage, No Boroughmongering, and No Corn Laws. Hulton and the Regency Tories refused the masses their political rights, and also expected many of them to acquiesce in near starvation caused by the deep post-war economic depression.[186]

In the words of Robert Poole 'the reformers played out the role of unenfranchised citizens, presenting the government with the unanswerable physical presence of vast bodies of freeborn Englishmen and women assembled to proclaim their lost rights.' [187] There is little doubt that Orator Henry Hunt had come forward as a champion of the people's rights and he was well suited to appeal very effectively to the exited passions of the

---

[185] Tom Waghorn, 'Killing Field' in Paul Horrocks, (ed), *The Making of Manchester, Manchester*, (1999), p. 12.
[186] Donald Read, Review of 'Peteterloo: The Case Reopened by Robert Warmsley,' *History*, Vol., 55, (1970), pp. 138-140.
[187] Poole, *op. cit.*, p. 112.

crowd.[188] The majority of the crowd however, attended in the belief that the political reforms he proposed would persuade the government to look after their interests and relieve them from absolute poverty. The working-classes attributed their poverty to large scale unemployment, low wages and high food prices, which they ' blamed upon a corrupt political system and the favours it showed on those that controlled it, especially the aristocracy and clergy.' [189]

The Reform meeting was held under the surveillance of the Select Committee of Magistrates, responsible for policing the day's events in Manchester on 16th August 1819. They included the Reverends William Hay, Charles Wickstead Ethelston, and the Reverend Mallory, James Norris, Colonel Ralph Fletcher, Mr Richard Marsh, Mr J. Sylvester, Thomas Tatton, William Hulton, Mr Wright, Mr Marriott and Mr Fielden. These men were a typical example of Britain's ruling class at this time. For example, William Hulton and Thomas Tatton were both large landowners James Norris was a barrister, and the Reverends William Hay, Charles Wickstead Ethelston and Mallory were Anglican Ministers.[190] In defence of the Special Committee of Magistrates, Michael Kennedy in his *Portrait of Manchester*, (1970), argued that:

When the great Radical meeting was called for on 16th August it is hardly surprising that the authorities considered the possibility that it represented a flashpoint for revolution

---

[188] Prentice, *op. cit.*, p. 146.
[189] Bush, *op. cit.*, p. 1.
[190] Frank Musgrove, *The North of England-A History of Roman Times to the Present*, Oxford, (1990), p. 274.

and that property in Manchester might be destroyed or damaged.[191]

---

[191] Kennedy, *op. cit.*, p. 67.

Saddleworth Museum and Art Gallery

Saddleworth Museum and Art Gallery

There is no doubt that the Select Committee of Magistrates were alarmed at the size and the discipline of the massive crowd who had assembled on St Peter's Field.[192] Some of the contingents were singing Methodist songs and it was more like a 'revival meeting than a revolution.' Nevertheless the Magistrates were determined to break up the meeting. [193] However, if the aim of the Radical organisers was to 'frighten the authorities rather than persuade,' then perhaps they succeeded only too well.[194]

On the 16th August 1819 the Radical contingents were closely watched by government spies.[195] However, the Radical organisers were aware of this and knew that the Manchester authorities were waiting for a 'pretext to use their muscle.' As a result they had taken precautions to ensure that the meeting would be a peaceful one.[196] When Hunt heard that preparations for the Manchester meeting had involved secret drilling on the moors with pikes and even firearms, he demanded that the Lancashire radicals 'cease playing soldiers' and stressed that they come to the meeting 'armed with no other weapon but that of a self-approving conscience.' [197] On 11th August Hunt issued *An Address to the Reformers of Manchester and its Neighbourhood* which read as follows:

You will meet on Monday next, my friends, and by your steady, and temperate deportment, you will convince your

[192] Thompson, *op. cit.*, p. 748.
[193] Schama, *op. cit.*, p. 133.
[194] Williams and Ramsden, *op. cit.*, p. 178.
[195] Read, *op. cit.*, p. 128.
[196] Schama, *op. cit.*, p. 133.
[197] Belchem, *op. cit.*, p. 9.

enemies, that you feel you have an important and imperious public duty to perform…The eyes of England, nay, of all Europe, are fixed upon you and every friend of real Reform and Rational Liberty, is tremblingly alive to the result of your Meeting on Monday next. Our enemies will seek every opportunity, by means of their sanguinary agents, to excite a Riot, that they may have a pretence for spilling our blood…Come then my friends, to a Meeting on Monday, armed with NO OTHER WEAPON but that of a self-approving conscience; determined not to suffer yourselves to be irritated or excited, by any means whatsoever, to commit any breach of the public peace.[198]

In fact Hunt had spent the week prior to the meeting in Manchester visiting the leaders of the radical contingents, to ensure that his instructions for peace and discipline were understood and would be strictly obeyed. On Saturday 14th August 1819 Hunt offered to surrender himself to the magistrates so that 'they should not have any pretence for interrupting the meeting.'[199] However, the magistrates declined his offer and instead began organising their forces of Yeomanry, Hussars, Infantry, Artillery and Special Constables to police the centre of Manchester.[200]

Later Samuel Bamford an organiser of the mass meeting in his *Passages in the Life of a Radical*, (1841), explained:

---

[198] Robert Huish, *The History of the Private Life of Henry Hunt Esq.* II, (London 1836), pp. 178-80.
[199] *Manchester Observer*, 28th August, 1819.
[200] Stevenson, *op. cit.*, p. 284.

> We had frequently been taunted by the press, with our ragged, dirty appearance…and the mob like crowds in which our numbers were mustered; and we determined…that we should disarm the bitterness of our political opponents by a display of cleanliness, sobriety, and decorum.[201]

Obviously Hunt's warning worked because the men, women and children arrived at St Peter's Field without weapons of any kind. Thompson stresses the fact that 'the presence of so many women and children was overwhelming testimony to the pacific character of a meeting which the reformers knew all England was watching.' [202] Not only were the reformers wearing their best Sunday clothes, they stood respectfully at one stage while the band played 'God save the King.' Anything less like a revolutionary meeting could not possibly have been imagined.[203]

The estimates of the crowd numbers differ considerably as is to be expected. For example according to the Magistrate Thomas Tatton, the total figure assembled was 30,000. Samuel Bamford on the other hand estimated 80,000, the *Manchester Observer* 153,000, *The Annual Register* 80,000, whilst *The Times* printed figures of 80,000 and later, 100,000.[204] William Hulton estimated 30,000.[205] Finally, Orator Henry Hunt and Archibald Prentice estimated 60,000, and this figure became the one generally accepted by historians.[206] However, I must agree with

---

[201] *Bamford Passages* I, *op. cit.*, pp. 176-77.

[202] Thompson, *op. cit.*, p. 752. *Working Class*

[203] A. H. Stamp, *A Social and Economic History of England From 1700 to 1970*, Guildford, (1979), p. 133.

[204] Marlow, *op. cit.*, p. 125. *Peterloo Massacre*

[205] Reid, *op. cit.*, p. 191.

[206] Marlow, *op. cit.*, p. 125. *Peterloo Massacre*

Alan Kidd who emphasises the fact that even the highest and lowest estimates represent the 'arithmetic of propaganda rather than reliable assessments of numbers,' but even the lowest estimate would suggest a crowd of unprecedented numbers for a meeting for the time.[207]

The meeting was expected to be a significant occasion. Therefore the Manchester newspapers and the reforming press from other towns were there in force. They included John Tyas from *The Times*, Edward Baines from the *Leeds Mercury* and John Smith from the *Liverpool Mercury*. Naturally Archibald Prentice and John Taylor from the *Manchester Observer* were also there.[208]

Archibald Prentice, watched the start of the meeting in St. Peter's Field from the window of a friend's house in Mosley Street, but he left the area to travel home just before the attack by the yeomanry took place. Some years later Prentice published his *Historical Sketches and Personal Recollections of Manchester*, (1851) recording what he had seen and heard on the day. According to his *eyewitness* account:

> The morning of the 16th of August came, and soon after nine o'clock the people began to assemble. From the window of Mr. Baxter's house in Mosley-Street, I saw the main body proceeding towards St. Peter's Field, and never saw a gayer spectacle. There were haggard-looking men certainly, but the majority were young persons, in their best Sunday suits, and the light coloured dresses of the cheerful tidy-looking women relieved the effect of the dark

---

[207] Kidd, *op. cit.*, p. 88.
[208] Ayerst, *op. cit.*, p. 18.

frustrations worn by the men. The 'marching order' of which so much was said afterwards, was what we often see now in the processions of Sunday-school children and Temperance societies. To our eyes the numerous flags seemed to have been brought to add to the picturesque effect of the pageant. Slowly and orderly the multitudes took to their places round the hustings, which stood on a spot now included under the roof of the Free Trade Hall, near its south-east corner. Our company laughed at the fears of the magistrates, and the remark was, that if the men intended mischief they would not have brought their wives, their sisters, or their children with them. I passed round the outskirts of the meeting, and mingled with the groups that stood chatting there. I occasionally asked the women if they were not afraid to be there, and the usual laughing reply was- 'What have, we to be afraid of? ' I saw Hunt arrive, and heard the shouts of sixty thousand persons by whom he was enthusiastically welcomed, as the carriage in which he stood made its way through the dense crowd to the hustings. I proceeded to my dwelling-house in Salford, intending to return in about an hour or so to witness in what manner so large a meeting would separate. I had not been home more than a quarter of an hour when a wailing sound was heard from the main street, and, rushing out, I saw people running in the direction of Pendleton, their faces pale as death, and some with blood trickling down their cheeks. It was with difficulty I could get anyone to stop and tell me what happened.[209]

---

[209] Prentice, *op. cit.*, p. 159.

The Reverend Edward Stanley, Rector of Alderly, who had private business to take care of in Manchester on 16th August 1819 with a Mr. Buxton, who owned the house which the Select Committee of Magistrates had chosen as their headquarters. Stanley remained there to watch the whole event from a window directly above the magistrates and later gave evidence that:

> I saw no symptoms of riot or disturbances before the meeting; the impression on my mind was that the people were sullenly peaceful.[210]

Robert Hyde Gregg the owner of Quarry Bank Mill, Styal, Cheshire a wealthy manufacturer gave evidence that:

> I saw Mr. Hunt's party...the conduct of the meeting was perfectly quiet and peaceable in every part...I felt no alarm.[211]

Robert Reid in his book *The Peterloo Massacre*, (1989), highlights the fact that prior to the meeting, Manchester and surrounding districts were practically under military occupation. The overall military commander Major-General Sir John Byng listed the full complement of troops under his command at this time:

---

[210] F.A. Bruton, *Three Accounts of Peterloo by Eyewitnesses, Bishop Stanley, Lord Hylton, Benjamin Smith*, Manchester, (1921), p. 21.

[211] Ann Brooks and Brian Haworth, *Boomtown Manchester 1800-1850, The Portico Connection*, Manchester, (1993), p. 81.

Military List and Muster Roll

Manchester	6 troops of Cavalry :	15th Hussars
	7 companies of Infantry	31st & 88th Regt.
Bolton	2 troops of Cavalry :	6th Dragoon Guards
Oldham	2 troops of Cavalry :	6th Dragoon Guards
Ashton	2 troops of Cavalry :	7th Dragoon Guards
Rochdale	2 companies of Infantry:	88th Regt.
Stockport	1 troop of Yeomanry Cavalry:(*CheshireYeomanry*)	
	4 companies of Infantry:	31st & 88th Regt.
Macclesfield	1 squadron of Cavalry:	(*Cheshire Yeomanry*)
	3 companies of Infantry :	31st Regt.
Altrincham And Knutsford		
	5 troops of Cavalry :	(*Cheshire Yeomanry*)
Warrington	3 companies of Infantry :	31st Regt.
Preston	1 troop of Cavalry :	15th Hussars
Blackburn	1 troop of Cavalry :	15th Hussars [212]

It must be noted that there is no mention of the Manchester Yeomanry Cavalry on Major General Byng's military list and muster-roll. This is because on the day of the meeting the Yeomanry were to be under the direct command of the Select Committee of Magistrates.[213] Sir William Jolliffe who rode in charge as Lieutenant of Hussars on the day later described the Manchester Yeomanry Cavalry as:

> Consisting of about forty members, who, from the manner they were made use of greatly aggravated the disasters of

---

[212] Reid, *op. cit.*, p. 141.
[213] *Ibid*, 141.

the day. Their ranks were filled chiefly by wealthy manufacturers; and without the knowledge possessed by a military body, they were placed unwisely as it appeared, under the immediate command and order of the civil authorities.[214]

We have been asked to believe that there had been no premeditation by the Select Committee of Magistrates to disperse the meeting by force and that the magistrates were only guilty of incompetence or ill-judgement and that everything happened by chance. An example of this view can be identified in J. Stevenson, in *Popular Disturbances in England, 1700-1870*, (1979), who argues,

> Whether the magistrates had intended all along to disperse the meeting once Hunt had arrived cannot be proved with certainty; at the very least they had acted with spectacular incompetence.[215]

Based on the evidence available this view should not be believed. Stevenson's view is also a view repeated in many documentary evidence. The Reverend Mr. Hay writing to the Home Secretary Lord Sidmouth on 7th October 1819, when attempting to justify his actions after Peterloo writes:

> The Committee continued to meet, and did so on Saturday [August] 14th Sunday, and Monday. Prior to the Saturday, different points had been discussed as to the propriety of

[214] Bruton, *op. cit.*, pp. 49-50.
[215] J. Stevenson, *Popular Disturbances in England, 1700-1870*, London, (1979) p. 284.

stopping the Meeting and the manner of doing so. They were of the opinion that Multitudes coming in columns with Flags and Marching in Military array were even in the approach to the Meeting a tumultuous assembly; and it was for a little time under consideration whether each column should not be stopped at their respective entrances into the Town, but this was given up-it was considered that the Military might then be distracted and it was wished that the Town should see what the meeting was, when assembled, and also that those who came should be satisfied they were assembled in an unlawful manner. Being satisfied....that in point of Law [the Meeting] if assembled as it was expected, would be an illegal Meeting, we gave notice to Lieut-Col L'Estrange....of our wish to have the assistance of the Military on the 16th. [216]

Perhaps it should be noted at this point that preparations by the Manchester authorities were very similar to those made the day before the Blanketeers meeting held in St Peter's Field in 1817.[217] The Reverend Hay's account is a clear statement of the Select Committee's intentions. It is also clear that the magistrates had a 'contingency plan' on 16th August 1819 for dispersing the meeting by force before it even started with the assistance of the Manchester Yeomanry Cavalry, regular armed forces and special constables.[218]

Finally the Magistrates contingency plan was put into action and the military forces were assembled. As planned Lieutenant

---

[216] E. P. Thompson, 'Thompson on Peterloo,' *Manchester Regional History Review*, Vol. iii, (1989), p. 74.

[217] Davis, *op. cit.*, p. 32.

[218] Thompson, *op. cit.*, p. 74.

Colonel George L'Estrange was the overall military commander on 16th August 1819. Directly under his command were 600 members of the 15th Hussars, several hundred members of the 31st and 88th Infantry Regiments and a detachment of the Royal Horse Artillery. His initial plan was to surround St. Peter's Field with his troops. The cavalry in the front line was to be used to disperse the crowd if the Magistrates decided this was required, whilst the Royal Horse Artillery were to be used as a last resort. However, the Yeomanry were under the immediate command of the Select Committee of Magistrates. [219] Sir John Byng, the overall commander of the military forces in the north of England was notably absent on the day, having a pressing engagement at a horse-race meeting.[220]

All reports agree that from early morning of 16th August, 1819 some 1500 soldiers were busily taking up their positions, like the Radical contingents. Completely unaware of the 'troop movements *surrounding* them,' the crowds waited patiently for Henry Hunt and the other speakers to arrive.[221] One Troop from the Manchester Yeomanry had assembled in Portland Street, whilst another had assembled in and around St John's Street along with a troop of the 15th Hussars and the Cheshire Yeomanry. Another detachment of Hussars and a troop of the Royal Horse Artillery with two six pounder field guns were stationed in Lower Mosley Street. In addition troops of the 31st Infantry Regiment were assembled in Brazennose Street, whilst a company of the 88th Infantry Regiment waited patiently in Dickenson Street.[222] In addition to the military two to three

---

[219] Bruton, *op. cit.*, pp. 49-50.
[220] Stuart Hylton, *A History of Manchester*, Chichester, (2003), p. 87.
[221] Marlow, *op. cit.*, p. 4. *Day of Peterloo*
[222] Thomson, *op. cit.*, p. 294.

hundred Special Constables had been recruited to police the day's events. The Reverend Stanley, in his *eyewitness* account declared that:

> In the centre [St. Peter's Field] were the hustings surrounded to all appearances by a numerous body of constables, easily distinguished by their respectable dress, staves and hats on....The chain from this main body was continued in a double line, two or three deep, forming an avenue to Mr. Buxton's house, by which there seemed to be free and uninterrupted access, to and from the hustings.[223]

At 10.a.m. the Select Committee of Magistrates first met at the *Star Inn* before moving on to Mr Buxton's house at 6 Mount Street overlooking St. Peter's Field arriving there by 11.00 a.m.[224] They assembled some thirty 'loyalists' citizens including Francis Philips who signed a sworn *affidavit* and the necessary arrest warrant for Henry Hunt and the other speakers was drawn up stating:

> Richard Owen [pawnbroker and special constable] hath this day made an oath before us, His Majesty's Justices of the Peace...that Henry Hunt, John Knight, Jos. Johnson, and – Moorhouse, at this time (now a quarter past one o'clock) have arrived in a car, at the area near St. Peter's Church and that an immense mob is collected, that he considers the town in danger.[225]

---

[223] Bruton, *op. cit.*, pp. 11-12. *Stanleys narrative*

[224] Horton, *op. cit.*, p. 5.

[225] *Manchester Observer*, 28th August, 1819.

John Edward Taylor the founder of the *Manchester Guardian* who witnessed the events at Peterloo recorded in his notes that:

> Early in the forenoon on August 16th persons supposed to be acquainted with the intentions of the magistrates distinctly asserted that Mr Hunt would be arrested on the hustings, and the meeting dispersed. I myself was more than once told so, but could not conceive it possible.[226]

At about 1.15 p.m. a carriage made its way across St Peter's Field with Hunt standing up in it. Mrs Mary Fildes, the President of the Manchester Female Reformers was also in the carriage. Whilst the female committee all dressed in white walked behind. At 1.20 p.m. Hunt arrived at the hustings which sparked off a great cheer from the crowd. At the same time reformer bands struck up 'See the Conquering Hero comes.' [227] In response, 'the Manchester Yeomanry Cavalry, the Special Constables, and the 'Loyalists' in general replied to the Radical cheer with one of their own.' [228]

At 1.35p.m. The Reverend Charles Ethelston made a feeble attempt to read the *Riot Act* from an upstairs window of Mr Buxton's house at 6 Mount Street as follows:

> Our Sovereign Lord the King chargeth and commandeth all persons being assembled, immediately to disperse themselves, and peaceably to disperse to their habitations of their lawful business upon the pains contained in the Act

[226] Thompson, *op. cit.*, p. 75. *On Peterloo.*, John Edward Taylor, *Notes and Observations, Critical and Explanatory on the Papers Relative to the Internal State of the Country*, (1820)
[227] Read, *op. cit.*, p. 131. Bruton, *op. cit.*, p. 14.
[228] *Ibid*, p. 135. Prentice, *op. cit.*, p. 161.

made in the first year of King George the First for preventing tumults and riotous assemblies. God save the King.[229]

Although it is highly unlikely that the crowd would have heard the Riot Act being read and a large number of witnesses later gave evidence to that effect.[230] Nevertheless, this procedure was required by law to give legitimacy to the military action that was about to follow.[231]

Then at 1.40 p.m. Orator Henry Hunt began to address the crowd. At this point a warrant was handed to Joseph Nadin, the Deputy Chief Constable of Manchester to arrest the speakers. Nadin argued that the special constables were not a strong enough force to execute the warrant without the assistance of the military. In order to assist Nadin mounted messengers were despatched calling for the assistance of the military and the Special Constables 'were ordered to withdraw from the field.'[232]

The messengers rode to Portland Street for the Manchester Yeomanry and to St. John's Street for the Hussars and the Cheshire Yeomanry. Reports generally agree that the Yeomanry first made their way towards the meeting along Cooper Street. It was here that the first fatality occurred when Mrs Ann Fildes, [not to be confused with Mary Fildes on the hustings] and her two year old son were both knocked down to the ground by the

---

[229] Brooks and Haworth, *op. cit.*, p. 80.
[230] Prentice, *op. cit.*, p. 164.
[231] Brooks and Haworth, *op. cit.*, p. 80.
[232] Read, *op. cit.*, p. 133.

Yeomanry and the little boy was killed, becoming the first casualty of Peterloo.[233]

Meanwhile Major Thomas Trafford, the Senior Officer commanding the Manchester and Salford Yeomanry Cavalry had taken up a position in Pickford's Yard nearby. Trafford was the first man to receive the order from the Select Committee to arrest the speakers on the hustings. He then ordered his second-officer-in command, Captain Hugh Hornby Birley a wealthy manufacturer who owned a mill in Oxford Road to carry out the order of the Magistrates.[234] All reports agree that the Manchester Yeomanry arrived first on the scene.[235] According to the evidence of Bishop Stanley the Yeomanry 'halted in great disorder, and so continued for a few minutes they remained on the spot. This disorder was attributed by several persons in the [magistrates] room to the undisciplined state of their horses, little accustomed to act together, and probably frightened by the shout of the populace which greeted their arrival.' [236]

The fact that the Manchester Yeomanry who were Tory partisans were the first on the field was the last link in the chain of events leading up to the Peterloo Massacre. These men were ardent in their politics, and had suffered from the taunts of the Radicals. There was also a feeling in the air that they were not likely to show much moderation in a crisis. In addition their prejudices had been further aggravated by the fact that during the morning of the 16th August, 'while gathering in the taverns

---

[233] Marlow, *op. cit.*, p. 4. *Day of Peterloo*
[234] Redford, *op. cit.*, p. 254.
[235] Bruton, *op. cit.*, p. 28.
[236] *Ibid*, p. 14. *Stanley's Narrative*

to have their boots cleaned and their horses curried, [currie combed] they had become half-drunk.' [237]

The Reverend Stanley in his eyewitness account describes the actions of the Manchester Yeomanry Cavalry as follows:

> Their sabres glistened in the air, and on they went, direct for the hustings. At first for a very few paces, their movement was not rapid, and there was some show of an attempt to follow their officer in regular succession, five or six abreast. They then soon increased their speed and with a zeal and ardour...seeming individually to vie with each other which should be first.[238]

At the same time the Yeomanry 'made a dash for the hustings, striking with their swords as they entered the crowd. Raw and untrained as they were, they were soon entangled and dispersed so that the chairman of the magistrates William Hulton later described them as ''completely defeated." [239]

According to Stanley's eyewitness account 'as the cavalry approached the dense mass of people used their utmost efforts to escape; but so closely were they pressed in opposite directions by the soldiers, the Special Constables, the position of the hustings, and their own immense numbers, that immediate escape was impossible. The rapid course of the troop was of course impeded when it came in contact with the mob, but passages were forced in less than a minute; so rapid indeed was it that the guard of constables close to the hustings shared the

[237] Read, *op. cit.*, p. 133, citing *The Whole Proceedings before the Coroner's Inquest at Oldham, c, on the body of John Lees*, (ed.), J. A. Dowling, (1820), p. 459.

[238] Bruton, *op. cit.*, p. 15. *Stanley's narrative*

[239] Redford, *op. cit.*, p. 254.

fate of the rest.' [240] Furthermore Stanley says 'one special constable, with a cut down his head, was brought to Mr. Buxton's house. I saw several others in the passage, congratulating themselves on their narrow escape, and showing the marks of sabre-cuts on their hats.'[241]

When the Yeomanry reached the hustings Stanley says 'a scene of dreadful confusion ensued. The orators fell or were forced off the scaffold in quick succession; fortunately for them, the stage being rather elevated, they were in great degree beyond the reach of many of the swords which gleamed around them. Hunt fell or threw himself-among the constables, and was driven or dragged, as fast as possible, down the avenue which communicated with the magistrates house; his associates were hurried after him in a similar manner.' [242]

On their way from the hustings to the magistrates' house, the prisoners were 'hissed and pushed by the Special Constables.' Moreover, a well known Loyalist in particular using a stick knocked Hunt's white hat down over his face. The Reverend Mr Hay was forced to address the Special Constables, 'urging them to restrain themselves.' [243] Stanley also says that:

> I saw nothing that gave me the idea of resistance, except in one or two spots where they showed some disinclination to abandon the banners; these impulses, however, were but momentary, and banner after banner fell into the hands of the military power.[244]

---

[240] *Bruton, op. cit.,* p. 15. *Stanley's narrative*

[241] *Ibid*, p. 19.

[242] *Ibid*, p. 16.

[243] Read, *op. cit.*, p. 139. citing *Memoirs of Henry Hunt*, III, London, (1820), pp. 617-19.

[244] Bruton, *op. cit.*, p. 18. *Stanley's narrative*

It was at this point the Hussars and the Cheshire Yeomanry came cantering up to Lower Mosley Street. The Cheshire Yeomanry rode along Windmill Street to the hustings and halted there. The Hussars lined up along Mount Street, in front of the magistrates' house, and awaited further orders. According to William Hulton when their commanding officer Lieutenant-Colonel L'Estrange asked what they were to do, the Chairman of the Magistrates William Hulton replied "Good God Sir! Don't you see they are attacking the yeomanry? Disperse the meeting." Thereupon the Hussars charged through the crowd from Mount Street to Deansgate using generally the flats of their swords, but almost 'inevitably sometimes using the edge of their swords.' [245]

Altogether eleven people, including two women, were arrested and imprisoned with Hunt as the main 'culprits of the day.' They were Johnson, Knight, Saxton, Healy, Moorhouse, Jones, Swift, Wild, Mrs Gaunt and Mrs Hargreaves. Thirty others were also arrested on minor charges. Richard Carlile was the only leading Radical on the hustings who was not arrested. After helping four women down from the hustings he escaped from the field and hid in a house nearby.[246]

At 8.45 p.m. on the evening of Peterloo, the senior magistrate the Reverend Mr Hay reported to the Home Office:

> The Riot Act was read, and the mob was completely dispersed, but not without very serious and lamentable effects…one of the Manchester Yeomanry, Mr. Hulme, was, after the parties was taken, struck by a brick-bat; he

---

[245] Redford, *op. cit.*, p. 254.
[246] Read, *op. cit.*, pp. 139-140.

lost his power over his horse, and is supposed to have fractured his skull by a fall from his horse. I am afraid he is since dead; if not, there are no hopes of his recovery. A special constable of the name of Ashworth has been killed – cause unknown; and four women appear to have lost their lives by being pressed by the crowd; these, I believe, are the fatal effects of the meeting. A variety of instances of sabre wounds occurred, but I hope none mortal; several pistols were fired by the mob, but as to their effect, save in one instance deposed to before Colonel Fletcher, we have no account. [247]

With the passage of time historical accounts of Peterloo vary. For example in more recent years E. P. Thompson highlighted the fact that Robert Warmsley in *Peterloo: The Case Re-opened*, Manchester, (1969),which he describes an apologist account on behalf of William Hulton, would have us believe that:

The Yeomanry were ordered to support the special constables in the execution of the warrant to arrest the speakers and then advanced in reasonable order and without aggressive intention or action into the crowd; and then that the crowd closed in upon them in a menacing manner and the Yeomanry were assailed, at some point close to the hustings, by brickbats and sticks hurled by a portion of the crowd, but that most of the Yeomanry kept their heads until Hunt and his fellow speakers had been arrested, and then, increasingly assailed by brickbats and

---

[247] Poole, *op. cit.*, p. 255.

hemmed in on all sides by a threatening crowd they were forced to beat off their attackers only using the flats of their sabres, in self defence.[248]

On the other hand Michael Kennedy in his *Portrait of Manchester*, (1970), without producing any evidence whatsoever in support of his claim asserts:

The Hussars drew their swords, held above their heads and moved into the crowd. In the melee, the crowd fled, some trying to unseat the riders and cut their girths. Against such actions the rider's only defence was to retaliate with his sabre.[249]

Obviously at the trial of Henry Hunt the Chairman of the Special Committee of Magistrates William Hulton was called as the chief prosecution witness.[250] He gave evidence that on 16th August 1819:

When the Yeomanry advanced to the hustings I saw bricks and stones flying. I wish to convey to the jury those stones and bricks were thrown in defiance of the military. I saw them attacked, and under that impression I desired Colonel L'Estrange to advance. On my saying to Colonel L'Estrange 'Good God, Sir, they are attacking the Yeomanry-disperse the crowd,' he advanced, and the dispersion of the crowd took place. Many of the people did

---

[248] Thompson, *op. cit.*, p. 68. *On Peterloo*
[249] Kennedy, *op. cit.*, p. 68.
[250] V. I., Tomlinson, 'Postscript to Peterloo,' *Manchester Regional History Review*, iii, (1989), p. 51.

not fly when the first body of the cavalry rode amongst them. The moment Colonel L'Estrange advanced with his squadron, the general flight took place.[251]

In contrast, John Tyas of *The Times* in his *eyewitness* account reported:

As soon as Hunt and Johnson had jumped from the wagon [hustings] a cry was made by the Cavalry, 'Have at their flags.' In consequence, they immediately not only dashed at the flags which were in the wagon, but those which were posted among the crowd, cutting most indiscriminately to the right and to the left in order to get at them. This set the people running in all directions, and it was not until this act had been committed that any brickbats were hurled at the military. From that moment the Manchester Yeomanry lost all command of temper.[252]

Captain Hugh Hornby Birley, a manufacturer and second officer-in-charge of the Manchester Yeomanry Cavalry did not dispute the attack on the flags. In his account he declared that, after the magistrates' warrant had been executed:

Considerable tumult prevailed, and a struggle ensued between the constables and those persons in the cart, who wished to save the caps of liberty, banners. Some of those who resisted were taken into custody, and the soldiers cut

---

[251] William Hulton, Evidence given at the trial of Henry Hunt.
[252] Thompson, *op. cit.*, p. 73. *On Peterloo*

with their sabres. In doing this, it was possible that some persons had been hurt, but not intentionally.[253]

On the question of the controversial stones and brickbats John Smith of the *Liverpool Mercury* gave evidence at Hunts trial that:

> I saw no stone or brick-bat thrown at them [Yeomanry] in my judgement, if any stones or brick-bats had been thrown I was in a situation likely to have seen it, my eyes and countenance were in a direction towards the military up to the moment of their reaching the hustings.[254]

The Reverend Edward Stanley in his eyewitness account also confirmed that:

> I indeed saw no missile weapons used throughout the whole transaction...but, the dust at the hustings soon partially obscured everything that took place near that particular spot.[255]

William Harrison, a cotton spinner in the crowd on St Peter's Field on 16th August 1819, later gave his *eyewitness* evidence at the inquest of John Lees in Oldham as follows:

Harrison: We were all merry in the hopes of better times.
Coroner: Were you not desired to disperse?

[253] *Ibid*, p. 73.
[254] *Ibid*, p. 73.
[255] Bruton, *op. cit.*, pp. 22-23. *Stanley's Narrative*

Harrison: Only with the swords-nobody asked us to disperse-only trying to cut our heads off with their swords...The soldiers began cutting and slaying, and the constables began to seize the colours, and the tune was struck up; they all knew of the combination. Amidst such music, few paused to distinguish between flats and sharps.

Coroner: Did they cut at you near the hustings?

Harrison: No, as I was running away three soldiers came down upon me one after another...there was whiz this way, and a whiz that way, backwards and forwards...and I, as they were going to strike, threw myself on my face, so that, if they cut, it should be on my bottom.

Coroner: You act as well as speak?

Harrison: Yes, I'm real Lancashire blunt. Sir, I speak the truth...whenever any cried out 'mercy,' they said 'Damn you, what brought you here.' [256]

Attention is also drawn to the evidence of Major Dynely, the commander of the Royal Horse Artillery and the two six pounder field guns held in readiness on the 16th August 1819 in Lower Mosley Street who writes:

> The first action of the Battle of Manchester is over...and I am happy to say has ended in the complete discomfiture of the Enemy....I was very much assured to see the way in which the Volunteer Cavalry knocked the people about during the whole time we remained on the ground; the

---

[256] Thompson, *op. cit.*, p. 73. *On Peterloo*; also see Joseph A. Dowling, (ed.), *Inquest on the Body of John Lees*, the *Whole proceedings before the Coroner's Inqest at Olham on the body of John Lees, who died of sabre wounds at Manchester*. Taken in shorthand with a plan of St Peter's Field., London, (1820)

instant they saw ten or dozen Mobites together, they rode at them and leathered them properly.[257]

Samuel Bamford, who was part of the crowd, described the scene immediately after the attack in his *eye witness* account:

In ten minutes from the commencement of the havoc, the field was an open and *almost* deserted place. The sun looked down through a still and motionless air...The Hustings remained, with a few broken and hewed flag-staves erect, and a torn and gashed banner or two dropping; whilst over the whole field were strewed caps, bonnets, hats, shawls and shoes, and other parts of male and female dress; trampled, torn and bloody. The Yeomanry had dismounted–some were easing their horses' girths, others adjusting their accoutrements; and some were wiping their sabres. Several mounds of human beings still remained where they had fallen, crushed down and smothered. Some were still groaning others with staring eyes were gasping for breath, and others would never breathe more.[258]

Sir William Jolliffe, Lieutenant of Hussars, described the scene after entering the Field in his *eye witness* account as follows:

An extraordinary sight: the ground was quite covered with hats, shoes, musical instruments and other things. Here and there lay the unfortunates who were too much injured to

---

[257] Marlow, *op. cit.*, pp. 148-149., citing Major Dyneley's letter, T.S. 11/4763/1055-56.
[258] *Bamford, Passages*, I, *op. cit.*, p. 208.

move away and the sight was more distressing, by observing some women among the sufferers.[259]

The majority of the panic stricken crowd running from St Peter's Field found it difficult to escape along the side streets because the main escape route along Peter Street was cut off by the 88th Infantry Regiment.[260] As a result the fleeing crowd were caught in a trap. In the words of Donald Read 'the fleeing mob found escape impeded by the presence of the military blocking their exit ways.' [261] In fact these troops had fixed bayonets, forming a line across the exit routes to the north side of town. Reports show that they inflicted serious wounds on the fleeing crowd either by 'stabbing with the ends of their bayonets or clubbing with their musket-butts.' Those that turned back found themselves under attack from the sabres of the cavalry. This incident was described by an anonymous *eyewitness*:

> The 88th troop were marched to a station at the south end of the Quaker Meeting House to interrupt the people[as] crowds passed who might fly in that direction and there indeed most dreadful slaughter to this quarter and were forced back by bayonets of the infantry, the cavalry cutting them in the rear.[262]

---

[259] Bruton, *op. cit.*, p. 55.
[260] Bush, *op. cit.*, p. 54.
[261] Read, *op. cit.*, p. 136.
[262] Bush, *op. cit.*, p. 54.

Another *eye-witness* account of John Railton appeared in the
Manchester Guardian on 18th August 1819, reporting a similar
thing:

> The cavalry were pursuing the mob and they were met and
> goaded by the infantry who were advancing upon and
> pricking them with fixed bayonets.[263]

The latest historical research has revealed that at least fifteen
entries in the casualty lists describe the injuries which were
caused by the 88th Foot Regiment. 'They show how the 88th
Regiment, stabbed people in the head, belly, back and arms with
their bayonets or clubbed them to the ground with the butts of
their muskets.' These entries relate to:

> William Batsan, John Boulter, John Brookes, Joseph
> Brookes, Thomas Buckley, Mary Evans, John Goodwin,
> John Hardman, Mark Howard, William Hurdies, William
> Moores, Joseph Ogden, John Pimblet, John Smithies, Peter
> Warburton.[264]

Sir William Jolliffe reported that on the 16th August 1819,
'Carriages were brought to convey the wounded to the
Manchester Infirmary.' [265] Newspaper accounts appeared the
next day Tuesday 17th August 1819, a reporter from the
Manchester Observer said that he saw 'Six coaches, three carts
and three litters loaded with the wounded travelling to the

---

[263] *Ibid*, p. 54; *Manchester Guardian*, 18th August, 1819.
[264] *Ibid*, p. 54.
[265] Bruton, *op. cit.*, p. 56.

Manchester Infirmary.' Another report in *The Star* newspaper on the 17th August declared that:

> All roads leading from Manchester to Ashton, Stockport, Cheadle, Bury and Bolton are covered with wounded stragglers, who have not been able to reach their houses after the events of Monday...There are 17 wounded persons along Stockport Road; 13 or 14 on the Ashton Road; at least 20 on the Oldham Road; 7 or 8 on the Rochdale Road, besides several others on the roads to Liverpool.[266]

At about 8.00 p.m. two troops of Hussars and two companies of the 88th Regiment were stationed in the New Cross area situated at the end of Oldham Street, Manchester. Sir William Jolliffe's says:

> Stones were thrown at the soldiers, and the Hussars many times cleared the ground by driving the mob up the streets leading from the New Cross. But these attempts to get rid of the annoyance were only successful for a moment...a town magistrate, who was with the picket, read the Riot Act, and the officer in command ordered the 88th to fire which they did by platoon firing down three of the streets...not more than thirty shots were fired; but these had a magical effect; the mob ran away and dispersed forthwith, leaving three or four persons with gunshot wounds.[267]

[266] Bush, *op. cit.*, p. 54; *Manchester Guardian*, 17th August, 1819, *The Star*, 17th August, 1819.
[267] Bruton, *op. cit.*, p. 58.

There is no doubt that many of those injured on St Peter's Field did not claim relief or seek medical treatment because their wounds were either slight or they feared victimization.[268] Archibald Prentice says 'hundreds of persons wounded upon that fatal 16th of August were enduring dreadful sufferings. They were disabled from work; not daring to apply for parish relief; not daring to ask for surgical aid, lest, in the arbitrary spirit of the time, their acknowledgement that they had received their wounds on St. Peter's Field might send them to prison, perhaps, to the scaffold.' [269]

Sir William Jolliffe gives an account of his movements on the day after Peterloo:

On the afternoon of the 17th I visited, in company with some military medical officers, the [Manchester] Infirmary. I saw there from twelve to twenty cases of sabre-wounds, and among these two women who appeared not likely to recover. One man was in a dying state from a gunshot wound in the head; another had his leg amputated; both these casualties arose from the firing of the 88th the night before. Two or three were reputed dead; one of them a constable, killed on St. Peter's field, but I saw none of the bodies.[270]

According to the entries in the 'Casualty Register Book' at the Manchester Infirmary on 16th August 29 people injured in St

---

[268] Thompson, *op. cit.*, p. 754. *Working Class*
[269] Prentice, *op. cit.*, pp. 166-167.
[270] Bruton, *op. cit.*, pp. 57-58.

Peter's Field had been admitted that day and two of these people had died. On the 17th 34 people were admitted and one of these people had also died.[271] On the question of casualty numbers at Peterloo as early as 1921 Bruton summarised that:

> It is a curious feature of the case that each side seems to be anxious to make its casualty list as imposing as possible. An interesting summary of the various estimates is given by MacDonnell in his *State Trials*. This summary includes the Official Report from the [Manchester] Infirmary, and the list of casualties to the troops. Without pursuing the matter further, we may say that a careful examination of the somewhat confusing evidence would seem to show that the estimate 'eleven killed and between 500 and 600 wounded' will not prove to be far wrong, provided that (1.) we understand 'killed' to include those who died of injuries received on the field; (2.) we include in the general total the casualties incurred during the disturbances some hours later in the neighbourhood of New Cross. At least one list, published subsequently, brings the total killed up to fourteen.[272]

The following year in 1922, G. M., Trevelyan in his article, *The Number of Casualties at Peterloo*, suggested that there should be full disclosure of the surviving casualty lists and that they should also be published.[273] His recommendations were largely ignored until 1989, when Malcolm and Walter Bee in

---

[271] Reid, *op. cit.*, pp. 190-191.

[272] Bruton, *op. cit.*, pp. 84-85.

[273] G.M. Trevelyan, 'The Number of Casualties at Peterloo,' *History*, VII, (1922), pp. 209-32.

their article *The Casualties of Peterloo*, compiled and re examined the lists as far as they were able. Producing a casualty figure of 630, the Bees showed that the number of those injured exceeded the previous estimates of about 400. They also showed that police and soldiers caused most of the injuries and not as previously asserted 'from being crushed in the crowd during the dispersal.' [274]

Finally however, Michael Bush in *The Casualties of Peterloo*, (2005), 186 years after Peterloo, put Trevelyan's recommendations into practice and by careful examination and analysis of all the lists, built on the work of Malcolm and Walter Bee. Bush emphasises that the principal evidence for the injured at Peterloo lies in the casualty lists compiled at the time or soon afterwards. There are *eight* surviving lists, six of which were completed by January 1820, a seventh by 1831 and the final one by 1844. Together these lists contain detailed information on the number of casualties, along with the names, addresses, occupations and ages of the injured, the nature of the injury sustained.[275] His vigorous reinvestigation has revealed that without a shadow of doubt there were 'at least 654 casualties, eighteen who died from their injuries.' and 'of the 654 injured 168 of these were women.' [276]

Malcolm and Walter Bee also drew attention to the fact that as early as 21st August 1819, Radicals meeting in London recommended that 'a subscription etc. in behalf of the Manchester Sufferers, should be made.' By October Radicals in Westminster and Southwark had each formed their own

---

[274] Bush, *op. cit.*, pp. 5-6.
[275] *Ibid*, p. 4.
[276] *Peterloo Casualty Lists*, in Bush, *op. cit.*, pp. 63-160., and for 'Peterloo Death List,' table see Bush, *op. cit.*, p. 45.

committees who later combined to establish the *Metropolitan and Central Committee Appointed for Relief of the Manchester Sufferers* and it was this committee who became the principal relief agency for the victims of Peterloo. They collected subscriptions and also received the subscriptions from other provincial appeals.[277]

In the meantime the journalist Archibald Prentice and his group of respectable middle-class reformers had established a local committee in Manchester.[278] However, at the beginning of November the Metropolitan and Central Committee sent a deputation to assist the Manchester Committee. During the next six weeks members of this deputation visited around 500 claimants in their homes during which time they 'kept a journal of the names, residences, ages, professions, number of family, extent and nature of the injury, if any, and what pecuniary relief each sufferer had received.' [279] The deputation from London also reported:

> In no one instance among the weavers did your Deputation see a morsel of animal food, and they ascertained that in most families where there were children the taste of meat was unknown from one year to another, and Six shillings a week was the average wage of an able-bodied and industrious weaver. Many could not get this. [280]

[277] Malcolm and Walter Bee, 'The Casualties of Peterloo,' *Manchester Regional History Review*, Vol. iii, (1989), pp. 43-44.

[278] Turner, *op. cit.*, p. 266.

[279] Malcolm and Walter Bee, *op. cit.*, pp. 43-44.

[280] Bruton, *op. cit.*, p. 84.

By February 1820 a grand total of £3,408 in subscriptions had been collected by the Relief Committee. Most of the subscriptions had been collected in the larger towns including Manchester, Liverpool, Birmingham, and London but many of the smaller provincial centres contributed also. However, 42 per cent of the subscriptions went on legal and administrative costs.[281] In addition "The Committee paid out £710 on account of the Trial at York; the Manchester Committee voting £100 for the same object." [282] Moreover only 31 per cent of the subscriptions that were collected were actually paid to the injured and over 80 per cent of the payments that were made amounted to £2 or less. Whilst those payments amounting to £5 or over were payed to only 3 per cent of those injured. The pathetic amounts of payments made to the suffers only added insult to injury.[283] The following extracts from the casualty lists illustrate the seriousness of some of the injuries and the amount of compensation received:

Lees, John, Oldham: sabred. Killed. A Coroner's Inquest on the body adjourned without a verdict. He is a rover [i.e. spinner] by occupation, working in his father's factory.

Fildes, Ann, Mrs, of 3 Comet-street: aged 27 with 5 children. Beat about the head by constables when escaping from the hustings. Her house was searched by Police, and she was obliged to leave home for a fortnight. £4 received in relief.

---

[281] Bush, *op. cit.*, p. 55-56.
[282] Bruton, *op. cit.*, p. 85.
[283] Bush, *op. cit.*, pp. 55-56.

Fletcher, John, Eccles: aged 31 and a weaver with 4 children. Thrown down and trampled on by Yeomanry horses; knee hurt and body crushed. 1 week disabled. 11/- received in relief.

Johnson, Margaret, Back of 24, Fawcett-street [Manchester] aged 27 with 3 children. Knocked down, beat by constables truncheons. 8 days disabled. £1 received in relief.

Taylor, Jonathan, High Knowles, near Lees: aged 29 and a weaver with 2 children. Sabre-cut on his nose and upper lip by a Yeoman, the toenails of his right foot trod off by cavalry horse. 3 weeks disabled. £1.10.0, received in relief.
[284]

The majority of the cases investigated by the Relief Committee related to the side of the Reformers. However, the 'loyalist' side claimed to have serious injuries casualties also. For example Francis Philips listed the casualties to the military personnel. In addition a subscription list was opened for the families of the Special Constables and apparently that appeal met with a generous response.[285]

There is no doubt that some members of the civil and military authorities were also injured. For example 'one special constable was killed.' The 15th Hussars reported that 2 officers and 21 other ranks were injured as the result of stone throwing or being hit by sticks. Whilst the Manchester and Salford Yeomanry named 3 officers and 41 other ranks sustaining injuries of a

---

[284] *The Peterloo Casualty Lists*, in Bush, *op. cit.*, pp. 63-160.

[285] Bruton, *op. cit.*, p. 84.

similar nature.[286] The Cheshire Yeomanry reported 4 men injured 'one of them dangerously.' [287] The names of the special constables injured included:

> John Ashworth (killed by sabre); James Chesworth (sabred), Robert Derbyshire (sabred), William Evans (trampled and dying), Henry Roggatt (sabred), Samuel McFadden (trampled), Mr Petty (trampled), John Routledge (trampled and nearly killed) [288]

The popular belief that only 11 people were killed and only 400 injured has been disproved by recent research that has established that there were 'at least 654 casualties, 18 of whom died of their injuries.' [289] However, when we examine the historiography of Peterloo we find that as early as 1923 Trevelyan highlighted the fact that 'Mr. Temperley's admirable chapter in Vol. X of the *Cambridge Modern History* p. 581, stated ''The result was the 'Manchester Massacre,' or 'Battle of Peterloo,' one man was killed and some 40 were wounded.'' [290] In more recent years Michael Kennedy in his *Portrait of Manchester* (1970) writes:

> No one knows the exact casualty figure. Hunt always said that fourteen were killed and 648 wounded, but the truth

---

[286] Reid, p. 193, citing English mss. 1/25a, summary of Casualties of Troops on 16th August 1819.
[287] *Ibid*, p. 193, citing HO 42. 192. Lloyd to Hobhouse, August 18th 1819.
[288] Bush, *op. cit.*, p. 61.
[289] *Ibid*, Preface.
[290] Trevelyan, *op. cit.*, p. 201.

seems to be nearer six dead (who included two of those on the side of authority) and about 30 hurt.[291]

The assertions by Temperley that only 'one man was killed and only forty were injured' along with those made by Kennedy that only 'six were killed and only 30 were hurt,' do not bear scrutiny.

The popular belief that only 11 people were killed and 400 were injured was largely developed by Donald Read in *Peterloo: The 'Massacre' and its Background*, (1958), and his figures have simply been copied into many histories. [292] For example, John Stevenson in *Popular Disturbances in England 1700-1832*, (1979), citing Read says 'Within ten or fifteen minutes 11 people had been killed and 400 injured.' Asa Briggs in *The Age of Improvement 1783-1867*, (1979), says 'eleven people were killed and over 400 wounded.' [293] Howard Martin in *Britain in the 19th Century*, (1996), says 'eleven were killed and 400 injured.' [294] Stuart Hylton in *A History of Manchester*, (2003), puts the number at 'eleven dead and about 420 wounded.' [295] However, there are dozens of similar examples.

The popular belief that most of the injuries were caused by the fleeing crowd is not supported by the evidence. This myth began with Sir William Jolliffe, a lieutenant in the 15th Hussars who had taken part in the dispersal of the crowd, who later said that:

---

[291] Kennedy, *op. cit.*, p. 68.
[292] Read, *op. cit.*, p. 139.
[293] Briggs, *op. cit.*, p. 210.
[294] Howard Martin, *Britain in the 19th Century*, London, (1996), p. 45.
[295] Hylton, *op. cit.*, p. 89.

Beyond all doubt...the far greater amounts of injuries were from the pressure of the routed multitude.[296]

This myth was further developed by Donald Read in his *Peterloo*, (1958), in which he makes the point that 60,000 were dispersed in ten minutes, and says:

> little wonder that hundreds were hurt, and many more by crushing than by sabring...with the exception of 140 cut by sabring many more were crushed or thrown down as a result of the pressure of the crowd. [297]

Read's assertion has been repeated in many histories. Although Michael Kennedy in his *Portrait of Manchester*, (1970), writes 'Most of the casualties were caused by panic, and several people were trampled to death by their fellows. No one knows the exact casualty figure.' [298] Norman Gash in *Aristocracy and People*, (1979), also asserts that 'Possibly half the deaths, probably even more of the non-fatal injuries, were among those who were trampled underfoot by horses and the crowd in the panic that ensued.' [299] More recently by Alan Kidd, in his *History of Manchester*, (2002), asserts:

> It was their rapid clearance of the crowd which caused most of the injuries, many of the wounded being trampled on or crushed in the panic of the dispersal.[300]

---

[296] Bruton, *op. cit.*, p. 53.
[297] Read, *op. cit.*, p. 140.
[298] Kennedy, *op. cit.*, p. 68.
[299] Norman Gash, *Aristocracy and the People Britain 1815-1865*, London, (1979), p. 95.
[300] Kidd, *op. cit.*, p. 94.

The recent research of Michael Bush has also revealed that 'many more injuries were caused by weapons' than were crushed by the fleeing crowd. He also argues:

> that the military and police deliberately inflicted severe injuries, both on the field and in the surrounding streets, attacking women, men, children and the elderly without respect for sex or age. Though the crowd was unarmed and unresisting they proceeded ruthlessly and with brutality in a sustained onslaught that lasted much longer than was necessary to fulfil their appointed task of clearing the field. Its real purpose was to teach a salutary lesson by terror and humiliation. [301]

The popular belief that the Hussars only used the flats of their swords is not supported by the evidence. For example Alan Kidd in his book *Manchester*, (2002), asserts 'the Hussars reportedly used only the flats of their swords' [302] In marked contrast the *eyewitness* account of Sir William Jolliffe who rode in charge as Lieutenant of Hussars on the day later recorded:

> The Hussars generally drove the people forward with the flats of their swords, but sometimes, as is almost inevitably the case when men are placed in such situations, the *edge was used*, both by the Hussars, and as I have heard by the yeomen, but of this later part, I was not cognizant; and believing though I do that nine out of ten of the sabre wounds were caused by the hussars, I must still consider

[301] Bush, *op. cit.*, p. 52.
[302] Kidd, *op. cit.*, p. 89.

that it redounds to the human forbearance of the men of the 15th. That more wounds were not received, when the vast numbers are taken into consideration with whom they were brought into hostile collision. [303]

Most recently Michael Bush highlights the fact that other entries in the casualty lists, show the Hussars acting with the same brutality as the yeomanry. For example the *eyewitness* account of John Fell, a Manchester shopkeeper says that:

The Hussars dispersed themselves in all directions, not in line and cutting the same as the others [Yeomanry] had done. [304]

Generally the Hussars were seen as more restrained than the Yeomanry. Several reports indicate that members of the Hussars were also seen as acting with restraint and even of intervening to protect people against the vicious attacks of the Yeomanry and the Special Constables.[305] A good demonstration of this restraint shown by the Hussars was the case of Elijah Ridings, among the crowd at Peterloo, who escaped injury through the help of an officer of the Hussars who called out to him, 'Be quick young man; this way,' pointing out to him a way of escape with his sabre.[306] In fact Hunt himself stated in a letter to the *Manchester Observer* on 6th September, 1819, that the massacre 'would have been worse,' but for the regulars 'who were heard to

---

[303] Bruton, *op. cit.*, p. 53.
[304] Bush, *op. cit.*, p. 53.
[305] *Ibid*. p. 52.
[306] Swindles, *op. cit.*, p. 187; Elijah Ridings, *The Vill, age Muse, Containing The Complete Poetical Works of Elijah Ridings*, Macclesfield, (1854), p. 8.

threaten these cowardly fellows with summary justice if they did not desist from cutting down the fleeing people.' [307]

Michael Bush draws attention to the fact that 'the perception of the event as a *massacre*, however, has been questioned in view of the small number of injuries resulting in death.' [308] For example Robert Walmsley in *Peterloo: The Case-reopened*, (1969), has offered the revisionist argument that 'Peterloo constituted an unfortunate tragedy rather than a *massacre*.' [309] A similar view is expressed by Norman Gash in *Aristocracy and the People, Britain 1815-1865*, (1979), who says 'Peterloo was a blunder, it was hardly a massacre.'[310] Donald Read, in *Peterloo: The 'Massacre' and its Background* (1957), identifies Peterloo as a massacre but writes in the Preface to his book:

> The successful designation of Peterloo as a 'massacre' represents another piece of successful propaganda. Perhaps only in peace-loving England could a death-roll of only eleven persons have been so described.[311]

On the other hand, E. P. Thompson in *The Making of the English Working Class*, (1963), says 'It really was a massacre.' [312] Joyce Marlow in her book *The Peterloo Massacre*, (1970), writes 'Hardly a massacre! Yes and No. The definition of a *massacre* is general slaughter or carnage which was what occurred on Saint Peter's Field.' [313] Michael Kennedy a

---

[307] Bush, *op. cit.*, p. 52. *Manchester Observer*, 6ᵗʰ September, 1819.
[308] *Ibid*, p. 42.
[309] Kirk, *op. cit.*, p. 61.
[310] Gash, *op. cit.*, p. 95.
[311] Read, *op. cit.*, p. vii.
[312] Thompson, *op. cit.*, p. 752. *Working Class*
[313] Marlow, *op. cit.*, p. 151.

journalist with the *Daily Telegraph* in his article 'What really happened at Peterloo?' writes 'It was certainly no massacre by any standard.'[314] This was followed by his *Portrait of Manchester*, (1970), in which he says 'It was certainly no massacre, as the term would usually be understood.' [315] Most recently Michael Bush argues that:

> In showing that most injuries were inflicted by the military and police and how deaths and severe injuries resulted from sabring, bayoneting and truncheoning of unarmed people, they render the term 'massacre'- though technically an overstatement in that Peterloo did not witness a large number of killings-an appropriate expression which encapsulates the enormity of what actually happened.[316]

The popular belief that the Irish population of the Manchester region did not become integrated with the Reform Movement is unsupported by the evidence. This notion was largely developed by E. P. Thompson who believed that:

> 'while sympathising with the agitation of 1816-20,' Manchester's Irish population 'did not become integrated with the movement.' [317]

Thompson's assessment has been proved to be incorrect. To begin with one of the most notorious districts of Manchester was 'little Ireland' where the Irish community lived on the banks of

---

[314] *Daily Telegraph*, 16th August, 1969.
[315] Kennedy, *op. cit.*, p. 68.
[316] Bush, *op. cit.*, p. 44.
[317] Thompson, *op. cit.*, pp. 707-8. *Working Class*

the River Medlock many of whom attended the meeting.[318] There is also evidence that Irish-handloom weavers from Newtown[Newton Heath] situated just outside Manchester also attended the reform meeting in St. Peter's Field on the 16th.[319] Finally however, Michael Bush has demonstrated that large numbers of Irish did attend the meeting and, in so doing, demonstrated a deep commitment to the cause of the reform movement. Because at least ' 97 of the recorded casualties were of Irish extraction, either immigrants from Ireland, or born in England of Irish parents-against 19 Welsh and one or two Scots.' [320] Many of the Irish who were injured at the Peterloo meeting also appear in the casualty lists for example:

> **Kelly, John**, 10 Clowes-street, Salford: aged 33 and a weaver with 2 children. Sabre-cut over his left eye, two inches long. He fell and was trampled on by the crowd. 5 weeks disabled. Spit blood for some time. £2 received in relief.
> **Mclone, Thomas**, Short-street, Bolton: thrown down and trampled on. Eye hurt. 10/- final.
> **McKenna, Mary**, 16 Nicholas Street [Manchester]: an interesting girl much bruised in the back part of the head by being trampled on. 40/- final [£2 more in pencil]. Manchester Committee 20/-.[321]

To summarise a massive crowd attended the reform meeting at St. Peter's Field which included a high proportion of women and

---

[318] Briggs, *op cit.*, p. 92. *Victorian Cities*
[319] *Bamford Passages, op. cit.*, I, p. 202.
[320] Bush, *op. cit.*, p. 28.
[321] *The Peterloo Casualty Lists* in Bush, *op. cit.*, pp. 63-160.

children. None of them were armed and their conduct was peaceable. The Select Committee of Magistrates was obviously nervous before the event and alarmed at the size and discipline of the crowd. They ordered the Manchester Yeomanry to arrest the speakers on the hustings immediately after the meeting began. The unrestrained Manchester Yeomanry did not confine themselves to seizing the speakers but instead, wielding their sabres, made a deliberate and general attack on the crowd. William Hulton, the Chairman of the Select Committee of Magistrates, then ordered the 15th Hussars and the Cheshire Yeomanry to rescue the Manchester Yeomanry and disperse the crowd. Evidence was presented in this Chapter to show that within the space of 10 minutes St Peter's Field was cleared except for the bodies of the dead and injured.[322]

The popular belief that there had been no premeditation by the Select Committee of Magistrates to disperse the meeting by force and that the magistrates were only guilty of incompetence or ill-judgement and everything happened by chance is contradicted by the evidence. In fact two days before the meeting the Reverend Mr Hay stated that magistrates were satisfied that the meeting 'if assembled as it was expected, would be an illegal Meeting.' [323] Therefore, although the magistrates had no power to prohibit the meeting beforehand, they assumed that it would turn out to be illegal and made plans to disperse it by the use of civil and military force.[324] The forces were assembled and warrants were issued to arrest the speakers before the meeting began. The popular belief developed that

---

[322] *Bamford Passages*, I, *op. cit.*, p. 208.
[323] Thompson, *op. cit.*, p. 74.
[324] Redford, *op. cit.*, p. 252.

most of the injuries were caused by the fleeing crowd is simply a myth. Evidence in this Chapter has shown that most of the injuries were caused by the use of sabres, truncheons, and the use of cavalry rather than by the crowd itself. The belief that the 15th Hussars only used the flats of their swords is equally fanciful. Evidence has demonstrated that, although the Hussars showed more restraint than the Yeomanry, with the majority using the flats of their swords to disperse the crowd, a small number used the cutting edges which inflicted serious wounds. In the same way the belief that only 11 people were killed and 400 injured has been disproved by recent research that has established that there were 'at least 654 casualties, 18 of who died of their injuries.' Finally, the belief that Manchester's Irish Population did not become integrated into the movement for parliamentary reform is also unfounded. Evidence was presented in this Chapter has shown that at least '97 of the injuries recorded in the casualty lists of Peterloo were to persons of Irish extraction, either immigrants from Ireland or those born in England of Irish parents.'[325]

In conclusion on 16th August 1819, a massive crowd had gathered in St Peter's Field peacefully and carrying no weapons to put pressure on the government to bring about parliamentary reform. Yet in spite of these factors and on the orders of the Select Committee of Magistrates were 'attacked by soldiers with sabres and bayonets, and by police with truncheons and staves. The outcome was at least 654 casualties, eighteen of whom died of their injuries.' This latest historical research has revealed that there is no doubt that these injuries were inflicted by the

---

[325] Bush, *op. cit.*, p. 28.

authorities quite deliberately. The fact that the military and police attacked an unarmed crowd of civilians, including women and children, both in St Peter's Field and in the streets surrounding it, goes to show that their real intention was to teach these people a terrifying and unforgettable lesson.[326]

---

[326] *Ibid*, p. 52.

Chapter Three

The Aftermath of Peterloo

The Borough reeves and Constables of Manchester and Salford do hereby caution all the inhabitants to close their houses, shops, and warehouses, and to keep themselves and all persons under their control within doors, otherwise their lives will be in danger. Carts and all other carriages must be instantly moved from the streets, and other public roads.

11.00 a.m. 17th August 1819 [327]

Clear-headed assessments in the aftermath of Peterloo were a long time coming and although it became known as the Peterloo Massacre, the events in and around St. Peter's Field on 16th August 1819 were regarded by both sides with a great deal of passion. The reformers were regarded with fear and suspicion by the establishment, and treated accordingly. This treatment resulted in further agitation which in turn led to increased repressive government reaction.

In the aftermath of Peterloo John Edward Taylor later reported that: 'on the 17th of August, which was Tuesday and consequently the principal market day in Manchester for cotton goods. One of the constables came upon the exchange about eleven o'clock, and in the utmost agitation ordered that the room should be closed, and declared the town and neighbourhood in a state of open rebellion. The following hand-bill was also

---

[327] Taylor, *op. cit.*, pp. 188-189.

partially posted, but soon afterwards it was rapidly pulled from the walls':

> The Boroughreeves and Constables of Manchester and Salford do hereby caution all the inhabitants to close their houses, shops, and warehouses, and to keep themselves and all persons under their control within doors, otherwise their lives will be in danger. Carts and all other carriages must be instantly moved from the streets, and other public roads.[328]

On the day of Peterloo Archibald Prentice and John Taylor on hearing that John Tyas had been arrested, had written detailed accounts of the "massacre" and swiftly dispatched them to London. Prentice says 'our narratives appeared in print on the following day.' These accounts were corroborated by John Tyas following his release from custody.[329] On 23rd August 1819 a report in *The Times* declared, 'Manchester now wears the appearance of a garrison, or of a town conquered in war.' [330] On 24th August 1819, *The Times* reported that on the 17th a special constable was killed in the New Cross district of Manchester and that there were riots in both Stockport and Macclesfield that evening. 'On the 20th a mob in the New Cross district fought a pitched battle with the cavalry.' [331] Another account appeared in *The Times* also on 24th August describing the appalling conditions in the New Cross district:

---

[328] *Ibid.*
[329] Prentice, *op. cit.*, p. 163.
[330] Read, *op. cit.*, p. 143. *The Times*, 23rd August, 1819.
[331] *Ibid*, p. 142. *The Times*, 24th August, 1819.

It is occupied chiefly by spinners, weavers...its present situation is truly heart-rending and over-powering. The streets are confined and dirty; the houses are neglected, and the windows often without glass. Out of the miserable rags of the family...hung up to dry; the household furniture, the bedding, the clothes of the children and the husband were seen at the pawnbrokers.[332]

Meanwhile alarmed at the tone of the public opinion circulating in London after Peterloo, on 19th August, a public meeting was hastily called at the Manchester police-office where the magistrates and the soldiers received thanks from grateful members of the loyalist public before adjourning to the Star Inn.[333]

After the Star Inn resolutions a *Declaration of Protest* was circulated by the local middle-class Radicals. The declaration was signed by 4,800 people, claiming that the meeting convened on the 19th had been "strictly and exclusively private,' without any right of a public town meeting. Instead of approving the proceeding at Peterloo, the signatories declared that the Reform Meeting on 16th August at St Peter's Field had been ' *perfectly peaceable*; that Riot Act, '*if read at all, was read privately, or without the knowledge of a great body of the meeting.*' Therefore they expressed their '*utter disapprobation of the unexpected and unnecessary violence by which the assembly was dispersed.*' [334]

---

[332] Reid, *op. cit.*, p. 7.
[333] Prentice, *op. cit.*, p. 163.
[334] *Ibid*, pp. 163-164.

Following the *Declaration of Protest* two meetings were called by the middle-class Radicals in Manchester. The first meeting approved the document. The second meeting established a Manchester subscription fund to relieve the Peterloo sufferers. Those attending this meeting appointed a committee to lead Manchester's respectable reformers. These men included Edward Baxter, William Harvey, Archibald Prentice, Joseph Brotherton, John Taylor, John Shuttleworth and Richard Potter. Therefore the immediate effect of Peterloo was to encourage Manchester's respectable reformers and to make use of the growing number of middle-class sympathisers who were outraged by Peterloo.[335]

Meanwhile on the 19th August 1819 the Reverend Mr Hay travelled to Whitehall and later that day gave his account to members of the cabinet which included Lord Sidmouth the Home Secretary, the Duke of Wellington, Lord Castlereagh, Lord Vansittart and Lord Eldon.[336] The Home Secretary who was always nervously aware of the Government's dependence on the magistrates in times of unrest wasted no time congratulating them.[337] On 27th August he wrote to the Manchester magistrates, Major Trafford, and the military personnel serving under him conveying the Prince Regent's thanks for:

> The great satisfaction derived by his Royal Highness from their prompt, decisive and efficient measures for the preservation of the public peace.[338]

---

[335] Turner, *op. cit.*, p. 266.
[336] Reid, *op. cit.*, p. 190.
[337] Williams and Ramsden, *op. cit.*, p. 176.
[338] Prentice, *op. cit.*, p.166.

The fact that the Prince Regent approved this form of congratulation was completely in character; fears engendered by the French Revolution had made him terrified of any form of public disorder.[339]

In Manchester the Prince Regent's complements were returned in a Tory "Address to the Prince Regent," signed by about 1,400 citizens including magistrates, clergymen, bankers, merchants and tradesmen. The Address emphasised the dangerous temper in which the Radical reformers had made their preparations for "a formidable display...of the collective strength of the revolutionary cause," and recalled "the universal consternation which prevailed amongst the loyal and peaceable inhabitants of these towns, when they beheld their street thus suddenly inundated by gathering crowds, from various counties, and from every part of the surrounding neighbourhood." [340]

Robert Hyde Gregg the owner of Quarry Bank Mill in Styal, Cheshire and his wife's cousin, Francis Philips, both witnessed the Peterloo Massacre in 1819.[341] Francis Philips was a cotton manufacturer and a prominent member of both the Pitt Club and Tory party. Soon after Peterloo Philips published *An Exposure of the Calumnies circulated by the Enemies of Social Order and reiterated by their abettors Against the Magistrates and Yeomanry Cavalry of Manchester and Salford,* (1819), defending the behaviour of the Manchester magistrates and the yeomanry cavalry at Peterloo. At the same time the Tory newspapers continued to make excuses for the Manchester authorities praising them and the military for their conduct.[342]

[339] David Saul, *Prince of Pleasure, The Prince of Wales and the Making of the Regency*, New York, (1998), p. 391.
[340] Redford, *op. cit.*, p. 256.
[341] Brooks and Haworth, *op. cit.*, p. 81. *Quary Bank Mill and Styal Estate*, National Trust Booklet, (2008), p. 8.
[342]Turner, *op. cit.*, p. 266-268.

Although the promptness with which Sidmouth conveyed the Prince Regent's congratulations to the yeomanry and the magistrates fuelled national public outrage.[343] In fact the action of the Government in sending its thanks before instigating an inquiry aroused an outburst from the middle-classes who would have never even considered going to the Peterloo meeting.[344] On 27th August 1819 Richard Carlile wrote in *The Republican* :

> The massacre of the unoffending inhabitants of Manchester, on the 16th August, by Yeomanry Cavalry and Police, at the instigation of the Magistrates, should be a daily theme of the press, until the Murderers are brought to justice by the Law officers of the Crown.[345]

Soon afterwards Sir Francis Burdett presided over a large meeting in Westminster where a resolution was passed calling on the Prince Regent to order the prosecution of the Manchester magistrates involved. Protest meetings were held in many other towns but all attempts to bring the magistrates to account failed.[346]

After Peterloo the Regency Tories were still in command of the situation and saw themselves as the natural champions of law and order against the forces leading towards revolution and anarchy.[347]

---

[343] Wendy Hinde, *Castlereagh*, London, (1981), p. 253.

[344] Trevelyan, *op. cit.*, p. 189.

[345] Richard Carlile, *The Republican*, No1, Vol. 1, 27th August, 1819.

[346] T. J. Wooler, 'Sir Francis Burdetts Address To The Electors Of Westminster,' *The Black Dwarf*, Vol. III, (1819), Prentice, *op. cit.*, p. 166.

[347] Turner, *op. cit.*, p. 268.

Print commissioned and published Richard Carlile showing a
sympathetic view of the reformers themselves.
Manchester library and Information Studies: Manchester Archives and Local Studies

On 25th August 1819, William Hulton wrote to Lord Sidmouth informing him that there were 71 injured persons being treated at the Manchester Infirmary. Hulton added at the end of his letter that he and the Committee of Magistrates hoped that he would see this small number of casualties 'as a proof of the extreme forbearance of the military in dispersing an assemblage of 30,000 people.'[348]

Throughout Manchester and Lancashire, soon after Peterloo, there was talk of retaliation. The massacre was discussed in the public houses, chapels, churches, workshops and at home. Meanwhile Manchester was almost under martial law, due to rioting and rumours about people marching in military contingents from surrounding districts. Samuel Bamford later wrote of the 'grinding of scythes and old hatchets…screw-drivers, rusty swords, pikes and mop-nails.'[349] However, by the end of the month rumours of insurrection disappeared largely because of the overwhelming moral support the reformers received throughout the country.[350]

Demands for a public enquiry came from the four corners of the British Isles.[351] Nevertheless, despite these pressures, Lord Liverpool refused to hold an enquiry into the conduct of the magistrates, or into the behaviour of the yeomanry.[352] Instead the Government rejected demands for a full independent inquiry and adopted a policy of total support for the Manchester authorities 'in the hope that the reports of the Yeomanry

---

[348] Reid, *op. cit.*, p. 191. citing, HO 42. 192, Hulton to Sidmouth, 25th August 1819.
[349] *Bamford passages* I, *op. cit.*, p. 216.
[350] Thompson, *op. cit.*, p. 755. *Working Class.*
[351] Marlow *op. cit.*, p. 43. *Day of Peterloo.*
[351] Wendy Hinde, *op. cit.*, p. 254.
[352] Marlow, *op. cit.*, p 7. *Day of Peterloo.*

charging with sabres flashing into the peaceable demonstrators would soon pass from the public mind.' [353] Lord Liverpool summed up the government's attitude of qualified approval when he wrote to Lord Canning:

> When I saw the proceedings of the magistrates of Manchester on the 16th ult were justifiable, you will understand me as not by any means deciding that course which they pursed on that occasion was in all its parts prudent. A great deal might be said in their favour even on this head; but, whatever judgement might be formed in this respect, being satisfied that they were substantially right, there remained no alternative but to support them.[354]

Not only were demands for a parliamentary enquiry resolutely rejected. The Attorney and Solicitor Generals were 'fully satisfied' as to the 'legality' of the magistrates' actions. In fact the Lord Chancellor Eldon was of 'the clear opinion' that the meeting 'was an overt act of treason.' Furthermore he believed that 'a shocking choice between military government and anarchy lay ahead.' State prosecutions against the victims of the day commenced at once. Although the Manchester magistrates had initiated the policy of repression at Peterloo Lord Liverpool's Government endorsed it with every means at its disposal. For example Henry Hunt, John Cartwright, Sir Francis Burdett, Richard Carlile, Sir Charles Wolsley and James Wroe

---

[353] Malolm and Walter Bee, *op. cit.*, p. 43.
[354] Read, *op. cit.*, p. 183., also see W.R. Brock, *Lord Liverpool and Liberal Toryism*, Cambridge, (1941), p. 112.

of the *Manchester Observer* were only a few of those imprisoned or awaiting prosecution by the end of 1819.[355]

In November 1819, *The Official Papers Relative to the State of the Country,* were published by the government and included a selection the various letters of the magistrates to the Home Office and some depositions. These *Papers* were carefully selected and published in order to prevent a parliamentary enquiry. The information Lord Liverpool later admitted in private: 'may be laid safely, and much more advantageously, by the Government directly rather than through the medium of any committee.'[356] Nevertheless the newspapers kept the story going. *The Manchester Gazette* continued to discuss the meetings being held across the country in an attempt to have the 'aggressors identified and punished.' However, even when direct evidence could be produced against offenders the magistrates argued that there was not enough evidence to justify the issuing of arrest warrants.[357]

John Lees, a Waterloo veteran, was confined to a hospital bed for three weeks, before dying from the injuries inflicted by the Manchester Yeomanry at Peterloo. [358] However, the Oldham inquest upon John Lees was a 'turbulent and ill conducted affair' at which the radical reformers tried to furnish evidence leading to a verdict of 'wilful murder' against the Manchester Yeomanry Cavalry. At the inquest at least nine witnesses testified to seeing the Yeomanry cut at the people in the crowd with their sabres, on their way to the hustings. One witness Jonah Andrew was questioned by the Coroner as follows:

---

[355]Thompson, *op. cit.,* p. 750. *Working Class*

[356]Thompson, *op. cit.,* p. 70. *On Peterloo*

[357]Turner, *op. cit.,* p. 267.

[358] Marlow, *op. cit.,* p. 13. *Peterloo Massacre*

Coroner: At what pace did they come?

Jonah Andrew, (cotton spinner), I think it was a trot. It was as fast as they could get, and the constables were making way for them.

Q. Did you see them striking any one?

A. Yes; I saw them striking as they come along, and they struck one person when they were about twenty yards from me…they squandered to the right and left before they came to me…

Q. Well: What then?

A. Why they began to cut and hack at the people like butchers.[359]

Another witness, Elizabeth Farren testified:

Coroner: Do you know anything of the death of John Lees?

Elizabeth Farren: No, I do not.

Q. Then why do you come here?

A. Because I was cut?

Q. Where were you cut?

A. On the forehead. (Here the witness raised her bonnet and cap, as also the bandage over her forehead, and exhibited a large wound not quite healed)

The Coroner: I don't mean that, woman. Where were you at the time you were cut?

A. About thirty yards from the house where the Justices were, amongst the special constables.

---

[359] Joseph A. Dowling, (ed.), *Inquest on the Body of John Lees, the Whole proceedings before the Coroner's Inquest at Olham on the body of John Lees, who died of sabre wounds at Manchester.* Taken in shorthand with a plan of St Peter's Field. London, (1820), pp. 57-58.

Q. Were you cut as the Cavalry went to the hustings, or on their return?

A. I was cut as they were going to the hustings. I had with me this child, (shewing the child she held in her arms). I was frightened for its safety, and tried to protect it, held it close to my side with the head downward, to avoid the blow. I desired them to spare my child, and I was directly cut on my forehead.

Q. What passed then?

A. I became insensible. [360]

The counsel for the family of the deceased John Lees produced a number of other witnesses in support of their case. However, they were not allowed by the Coroner. On the other hand the counsel for the defence produced several witnesses including the Deputy Chief Constable, Joseph Nadin, who all contradicted the evidence.[361] Naturally this evidence was believed because the sympathy of the establishment had been demonstrated only a month after Peterloo. On 27th September 1819 it was reported in *The Times* that a clerical magistrate had used his position on the Bench to address the accused as follows:

> I believe you are a downright blackguard reformer. Some of you reformers ought to be hanged, and some of you are sure to be hanged-the rope is already round your necks.[362]

Radicals were angered by the obstruction of the John Lees inquest which was repeatedly adjourned and then finally

---

[360] *Ibid*, pp. 177-178.
[361] Thompson, *op. cit.*, p. 70. *On Peterloo*
[362] Thompson, *op. cit.*, p. 752. *Working Class*

discontinued in later in 1819 because of a technical irregularity. Apparently the coroner and the jury had not inspected the body at the same time however it became obvious that the coroner would have used any excuse to stop the inquest.[363]

After the John Lees inquest the focus then turned to Hunts trial along with the other organisers of the Peterloo meeting, which began at York on 16th March 1820. They were all charged with 'assembling with unlawful banners at an unlawful meeting for the purpose of citing discontent.' The *Manchester Gazette* printed over 23 columns about the trial over the following three weeks. Finally however, Hunt and most of the radical leaders were convicted even after a 'brilliant defence.' [364]

By the end of 1820 the majority of the leaders of the reform movement were in prison, including Sir Francis Burdett, Henry Hunt and Thomas Wooler editor of the *Black Dwarf.* [365] On the other hand the Reverend Mr Hay was rewarded with a living of £2,400 a year for his services in 'putting down' the Reformers.[366] Earl Fitzwilliam, Lord Lieutenant of the West Riding and one of the most respected of the Whig peers who called several country meetings in Yorkshire demanding an enquiry into Peterloo, was removed from his Lord-Lieutenancy for his part in protesting about the massacre.[367]

Lord Liverpool's Government had no other remedy but further repression.[368] The Duke of Wellington feared that a full scale insurrection was imminent and there was a general agreement in

---

[363]Turner *op. cit.,* p. 267.
[364] *Ibid.*
[365] Schama, *op. cit.,* p. 134.
[366] Prentice, *op. cit.,* p. 169.
[367] Williams and Ramsden, *op. cit.,* pp. 178-79.
[368] Clark George, Sir, *English History A Survey,* Oxford, (1978), p. 417.

Tory circles that the 'right of assembly must be curtailed.'[369] An extraordinary session of Parliament was called to approve an increase in the strength of the Army by 10,000 men and to introduce the Six (Gagging) Acts of repression.[370] The Six Acts represented a political rather than an economic response to distress and disorder. The ruling classes were firmly opposed to any change in the form of government, and most were convinced that concessions to the people would open the way for revolution.[371]

The Governments first proposal was the *Training Prevention Act*, intended to prevent drilling and training of persons in the use of arms; the second the *Seizure of Arms Act*, which gave justices in certain counties the power to search for arms and to arrest persons found carrying them for purposes dangerous to the peace; the third the *Misdemeanours Act*, intended to prevent delay in the administration of justice through the practice of traversing; the fourth the *Seditious Meetings Prevention Act*, designed to prevent the great Radical meetings. This Act prohibited all public meetings of more than 50 persons. The last two the *Blasphemous and Seditious Libels Act* and the *Newspaper Stamp Duties Act*, were both intended to restrict the influence of the Radical Press.[372]

The Whigs offered no opposition to the Act preventing civilians taking part in para-military activities, but they opposed the other five Acts. Nevertheless, all Six Acts passed with a comfortable majority. The issues these Acts raised polarised parliament into two distinct parties, those *for* and those *against*,

---

[369] Hinde, *op. cit.*, p. 254.
[370] Gregg, *op. cit.*, p. 93.
[371] Evans and Pledger, *op. cit.*, pp. 8-9.
[372] *Ibid.*

the Government's suppression of radicals. Furthermore these divisions were not confined to parliament. English society as a whole was divided with petitions, mass meetings, and demonstrations being organised by both sides in the debate about the action taken by the Manchester authorities.[373] The Six Acts, passed in the winter of 1819, were no more than an inevitable outcome of the policy previously adopted by Lord Liverpool's Government.[374]

There is no doubt that Lord Liverpool's government in its determination to control the nation, created the most repressive regime in modern British history.[375] The only aspect of the working-class Radical organisation which parliament did not control was the Union Society network.[376] There is also no doubt that even after the passage of the Six Acts the work of the spies and *agents provocateurs* continued, as there were still active reformers whom they could dupe and betray. A major assault against the 'seditious' and 'blasphemous' press, began right away. This was followed by a number of prosecutions against newsvendors and publishers, which were largely instituted by private prosecuting societies secretly funded by the government.[377]

The year that followed Peterloo and the Six Acts, was the year that the Prince Regent succeeded to the throne as George IV and when the Cato Street conspiracy took place.[378] In the shocked aftermath of Peterloo the radicals themselves divided into two

---

[373] W. A. Speck, *A Concise History of Britain 1707-1975*, Cambridge, (1995), p. 67.
[374] Trevelyan, *op. cit.*, p. 190.
[375] Reid, *op. cit.*, p.199.
[376] Read, *op. cit.*, p.187.
[377] Thompson, *op. cit.*, p. 768. *Working Class*
[378] Trevelyan, *op. cit.*, p. 191.

groups. On the one hand there were those like Hunt, who felt it was important to continue by lawful constitutional means and on the other the more aggressive group including men like Arthur Thistlewood who had been imprisoned after the Spa Fields riot and had finished his term in the autumn of 1819. He planned what came to be known as the Cato Street Conspiracy, a crazy scheme involving a plan not merely to assassinate the entire Cabinet but to attack the Tower of London, the Bank of England and even parliament.[379] On the night of 23rd February 1820, acting on 'information received,' Bow Street officers and soldiers raided a stable, with rooms above, in Cato Street, a small back street running parallel to the Edgware Road in London. They surprised a group of men and found a quantity of arms. In the scuffle one police officer was run through with a sword and killed.[380]

The Cato Street Conspiracy gave Lord Liverpool's Government the publicity it needed and Thistlewood's trial was made public in order to demonstrate that there had been a 'diabolical plot' to start a 'revolution' by assassinating the entire Cabinet. In April 1820 Thistlewood and a four of his accomplices appeared at the Old Bailey. Thistlewood did not deny the charges but claimed the he was motivated by 'concern for the welfare of his starving countrymen and indignation at such atrocities as Peterloo.' [381] In response, the *Manchester Gazette* published an article making it clear that Manchester men had nothing to do with the party of extremists led by Arthur

[379] Schama, *op. cit.*, p. 134.
[380] Thomas Jackson, *Trials of British Freedom*, London, p. 84.
[381] *Ibid*, pp. 84-85.

Thistlewood and his associates.[382] Thistlewood and four of his accomplices were hanged on the 1st May 1820.[383]

On 15th May 1821 Sir Francis Burdett made a speech in the House of Commons as follows:

> The pretence of the people having carried arms to the meeting was utterly groundless; and to talk of having commenced the attack upon the armed soldiers, was, on the face of it, absurd and ridiculous. The people knew they had no means of repelling the attack. They thought they had assembled under the protection of the law.

> The wretches who had perpetrated the massacre at Manchester were at the time in a state of intoxication. When they attacked sword in hand, the people fled, or attempting to fly, from the dreadful charge made upon them; but, to their horror and surprise, they found flight impracticable; for the avenues of the place were closed by armed men. On one side they were driven back at the point of the bayonet by the infantry; while on the other they were cut down by the yeomanry.

> An idea might be formed of the violent and indiscriminate manner of the massacre, when it was known that this yeomanry, in their fury and blindness, actually cut down some of their own troops; for the constables on that occasion were armed, and some of them had fallen under the hoofs of the yeomanry.[384]

[382] Turner, *op. cit.*, p. 273.
[383] Tevelyan, *op. cit.*, p. 191.

In April 1822 the campaign for justice after Peterloo continued with the trial of *Redford v. Birley* and others. Thomas Redford, wounded at Peterloo by a yeomanry sabre, began a civil action for assault against the yeomanry commander Hugh Hornby Birley, and three other yeomen 'Withington, Meagher and Oliver.' [385] However, unlike the John Lees inquest in Oldham *Redford v. Birley* was well organised. Thomas Redford's 'twenty-nine witnesses included; seven weavers, one fustian-cutter, one carver and gilder, two cotton manufactures, one pattern drawer, one Church of England clergyman the Reverend Stanley, one Unitarian minister, one Quaker surgeon, three gentlemen, one salesman, four journalists including John Tyas of the *Times*, Edward Baines from the *Leeds Mercury*, and John Smith of the *Liverpool Mercury*, one chemist, two householders with a house overlooking St Peter's Field, and one member of the Manchester Yeomanry Cavalry.'

In his defence Captain Birley called seventeen witnesses who included the Deputy Chief Constable Joseph Nadin, two of the Select Committee of Magistrates, William Hulton and the Reverend Mr Hay, 'one merchant's agent, one calico printer, one policeman, two lawyers, one gentleman, one farm steward, and at least six special constables.' [386]

At the trial twenty nine of Redford's witnesses swore that they did not see brickbats, stones or any other form of resistance by the crowd to the Yeomanry before they reached the hustings. In contrast, seventeen of Captain Birley's witnesses swore that they

[384] Burdett Sir Francis, Speech made to the House of Commons 15th May 1821.
[385] Turner, *op. cit.*, p. 271.
[386] Thompson, *op.cit.*, pp. 70-71.

did.[387] Finally, however, the jury accepted the defendant's plea that the assault had been lawfully carried out in the 'the dispersal of an unlawful assembly' and all the charges against the defendants were dismissed. [388] To add insult to injury, the defendants, costs were paid by Lord Liverpool's Government. Both Henry Hunt and the *Manchester Observer* claimed the trial was 'little more than a sham.' However, after *Redford v. Birley* the campaign for justice after Peterloo lost some of its momentum.[389]

Hugh Hornby Birley was promoted to the rank of Major was well rewarded for his service at Peterloo. He was also appointed as a magistrate and founded the Manchester Chamber of Commerce. Later on of course, he was appointed Deputy Lieutenant of the County Palatine of Lancashire.[390] In 1822 Birley's public work was recognised by several presentations. For example his grandson, the Reverend Hugh H. Birley, of Leamington, describes two of these presentations, the first:

> A beautifully engraved sword 'made by Joseph H. Reddell Sword Cutler to His Majesty's Hon. Board of Ordnance Balsall Armory near Birmingham.' The date on the hilt is 'March 10, 1822.' The sword bears the following inscription:- Presented to Hugh Hornby Birley Esq Major Commandant of the Manchester and Salford Yeomanry Cavalry by the Non Commissioned officers and privates under his command in testimony of their esteem for him as a Soldier and a gentleman.

---

[387] *Ibid.*
[388] Marlow, *op. cit.*, p. 7. *Day of Peterloo*
[389] Turner, *op. cit.*, p. 271.
[390] Brooks and Haworth, *op. cit.*, p. 83.

This was probably intended to show sympathy of the Yeomanry with Major Birley at the time of the case of *Redford v. Birley*. The second presentation was:

> A valuable piece of plate inscribed:- Presented to Hugh Hornby Birley, Esq., by members of the Chamber of Commerce and Manufactures of Manchester and other gentlemen, in testimony of the high consideration in which they hold his invaluable services as President of that Institution from the period of its formation in the year 1821 until 1828. Manchester, Oct.[391]

The religious life in Manchester was to change dramatically after Peterloo as it became dominated by a policy of loyalty to the establishment. For example only a month after Peterloo the Anglican Sunday School Committee called a special meeting to organise measures 'to prevent any of the Children from coming with White Hats or other Badges which are now used by the disloyal and disaffected as expression of their political sentiments.' Moreover at the time of Peterloo most of the working-class Methodists in Manchester were strong supporters of Henry Hunt and the Radical Reform Movement. However, after Peterloo Wesleyan Methodists prohibited the wearing of Radical badges. This was part of their policy of demonstrating loyalty to the establishment under the scrutiny of Manchester's ruling Anglican authorities. A year after Peterloo the Methodist Conference laid down a rule of non-association with the Radical Reformers. Methodists were instructed to follow their

---

[391] J. R. M. Albrecht, 'Major Hugh Hornby Birley,' in *Transactions of the Lancashire and Cheshire Antiquarian Society*, Vol. XL, 1922-1923, Manchester, (1925), pp. 197-198.

'occupations and duties in life in peaceful seclusion from all strife and tumults.' As early as November 1819, the Methodist Committee of Privileges expressed its 'strong and decided disapprobation of certain tumultuous assemblies which have lately been witnessed in several parts of the country.' [392] A delegation of lay Methodists told a Manchester circuit superintendent during the aftermath of Peterloo 'Methodist Preachers were as bad as the Church ministers in supporting the government.' [393]

The Roman Catholic Church in Manchester after Peterloo adopted a similar policy to that of the Anglicans and Wesleyans. On the 30th November 1819, the *Manchester Mercury* reported that 'all association with the Radical Reformers was forbidden from the pulpit on pain of excommunication.' However, the poverty-stricken Irish handloom weavers generally ignored this official policy largely due to the fact that the Radicals supported a programme of Catholic Emancipation and had helped them with their distress. In a similar manner the society of Quakers in Manchester also chose a policy of 'loyalty' after Peterloo. However, five days before Peterloo they had already dissociated themselves from a self-styled Quaker who had presided at a Radical Reform meeting at Leigh. The *Manchester Observer* declared its 'surprise and disgust' at their attitude. As a general rule none of the various churches suffered serious permanent losses to their congregations from defections to Radicalism.[394]

In the aftermath of Peterloo the great Radical popular movement which began in Lancashire in 1816 ended its days in

---

[392] Read, *op. cit.*, p. 201. *Manchester Chronicle*, 28th August, 1819. *Manchester Chronicle*, 27th November, 1819.
[393] Alan D. Gilbert, 'Religion and political stability in early industrial England,' in Patrick O'Brien and Roland Quinault, (ed.), *The Industrial Revolution and British Society*, Cambridge, (1993), p. 91.
[394] Read, *op. cit.*, pp. 204-205. *Manchester Mercury*, 30th November, 1819. *Manchester Obsever*, 21st August, 1819.

gradual decline. What had been the first large-scale political movement of the new industrial working-class did not achieve its aim. [395] Manchester's involvement in the reform movement reached its peak at Peterloo. However, Radical activity moved to the smaller textile towns like Accrington, Blackburn, Bolton, Burnley, Darwen, Oldham and Stockport whose communities had been radicalised by Peterloo.[396] For example, in 1826 following the severe depression of that year the power-loom riots broke out in these northern towns. On 24th April rioting broke out in east Lancashire which continued for three days. Altogether twenty-one mills were attacked and over 1,000 power-looms were destroyed. The soldiers were called in again and the magistrates swore in large numbers of Special Constables. During the night 20 ring-leaders were arrested in their homes and taken to Lancaster gaol.[397] In contrast Popular Radicalism in Manchester did not resurface again until the reform agitation of 1830-2.[398]

Lord Sidmouth the Home Secretary remained in Lord Liverpool's' Cabinet until he retired in 1824 and died at the age of 86.[399] Joseph Nadin was the Deputy Chief Constable of Manchester for more than twenty years and when he resigned in March 1821 and was succeeded by Steven Lavender from London. [400] By this time Nadin was a wealthy man and he bought a large property in Cheshire where he lived the life of the landed gentry until his death in 1848, aged 83.[401] In 1820

[395] *Ibid*, p. 162-163.
[396] Kidd, *op. cit.*, p. 97.
[397] Aspin, *op. cit.*, pp. 64-70.
[398] Kidd, *op. cit.*, p. 97.
[399] Hylton, *op. cit.*, p. 89-90.
[400] Harland, *op. cit.*, p. 195.
[401] Hylton, *op. cit.*, pp. 89-90.

William Hulton was offered a safe Tory seat in the House of Commons, but declined suspecting he would be the target of abuse during an election campaign. Nevertheless, in 1841, he stood as the Tory candidate for Bolton and during his election campaign he was attacked by the crowd. Although he continued to play a part in public affairs, he never lived the Peterloo Massacre down. Many years later whilst at a public house in Newton-le-Willows, William Hulton was reported to have said: 'It occurred to them [the Magistrates] that it was their duty to call up every friend of the Monarchy and the Church to counteract the machinations of the enemies of both.' [402]

Henry Hunt had been the foremost public speaker for the reform movement. He spoke at Spa Fields in 1816, and continued his activity during the suspension of *Habeas Corpus* in 1817, when William Cobbett thought it more politic to retire to America. As the main speaker at Peterloo, and was imprisoned for his part in the meeting.[403] On 29th October 1822 after serving two and a half years in Llchester gaol in Somerset he was finally released.[404] When Hunt and the others arrested were released, tens of thousands lined the route for their triumphant return to Manchester. Despite the urging of those who advocated an armed uprising, Hunt's popularity ensured that the majority accepted his peaceful and lawful methods.[405] Later on Hunt was elected as M.P. for Preston in 1830 to 1832, and he remained loyal to the demand for universal suffrage, attacking the 1832 Reform Act.[406]

---

[402] Thompson, *op. cit.*, p. 75. *On Peterloo*
[403] Thompson, *op. cit.*, p. 682. *Working Class*
[404] Marlow, *op. cit.*, p. 200. *Peterloo Massacre*
[405] Bush, *op. cit.*, p. 90-91.
[406] Thompson, *op. cit.*, p. 682. *Working Class*.

The memory of Peterloo remained a force in politics in Lancashire for many years after 1819 to encourage future reformers. When the Duke of Wellington visited Manchester in 1829 he was greeted by angry crowds waving placards with the words 'Remember Peterloo.'[407] A generation later the name Peterloo frequently invoked by the Chartist leaders, whose campaign was similar to that of the Peterloo Radicals. At the first great Chartist meeting near Manchester in 1838 the Peterloo banners were carried in the procession. In 1842 the foundation-stone of a Manchester memorial to Henry Hunt was laid by the Fergus O'Connor the Chartist leader.[408]

In conclusion although it became known as the Peterloo Massacre, the events in and around St. Peter's Field on 16th August 1819 were regarded by both sides with a great deal of passion. The reformers were regarded with fear and suspicion by the establishment, and treated accordingly. This treatment resulted in further agitation which in turn led to increased repressive government reaction. When it came to the question of public order, Lord Liverpool's Government and the local authorities were ferocious in suppressing discontent, as the story of Peterloo illustrates. It has been demonstrated in this Chapter that the first reaction of the Government to Peterloo was further repression, and the notorious Six Acts were passed soon after Peterloo. They were intended to prevent large public meetings, suppress the radical press, and undermine the whole movement for radical reforms.[409] Nevertheless, Peterloo was a turning point in British history this was largely because the working-class

---

[407] Marlow, op. cit., p. 200.
[408] Read, op. cit., p. 206.
[409] David Thomson, England in the Nineteenth Century 1815-1914, Harmondsworth, (1979), p. 40.

gained a great deal of middle-class sympathy and support for their cause. One example on hearing the news Shelley wrote *The Mask of Anarchy* and although the Government passed the notorious Six Acts to end all agitation it did not succeed and eventually came to see that blind repression of a disenfranchised people would never work.[410]

During the 1870's Ford Madox Brown wished to include a painting depicting the Peterloo Massacre in a series of frescos commissioned to decorate the new Manchester Town Hall. However, the committee responsible for selecting the ideas for the work considered the theme unacceptable, because Peterloo was still a political issue by the 1870's. Nevertheless, Peterloo inspired many contemporary prints and drawings including one vigorous satire by George Cruickshank. It was not until the New Free Trade Hall in Manchester was opened in 1951 that any of the public buildings contained depictions of Peterloo.[411]

One hundred and fifty years after Peterloo, Michael Kennedy highlighted the fact that the word Peterloo 'caused heated debates in Manchester City Council in 1969 when a proposal to re-name St. Peter's Ward Peterloo Ward, was not for the first time rejected.' [412] On 7th September 1972, an article appeared in the *Manchester Evening News* reporting 'The majority labour group on Manchester council last night gracefully admitted defeat in its attempt to rename Peter Street 'Peterloo Street.' Earlier, the Manchester stipendiary magistrate had upheld the objections of Peter Street traders to the change.' [413] However, a blue plaque was attached to the outside of the Free Trade Hall in

---

[410] Aspin, *op. cit.*, p. 61.
[411] *Ibid*, p. 208.
[412] Kennedy, *op. cit.*, p. 69.
[413] *Manchester Evening News*, 7th September, 1972.

1972. [414] This plaque merely recorded 'The site of St Peter's Field where on 16th August 1819, Henry Hunt, Radical Orator, addressed an assembly of about 60,000 people, their subsequent dispersal by the military is remembered as 'Peterloo.'' [415] More recently on the 188th anniversary of the Peterloo Massacre a group of campaigners gathered on the site to demand a new monument to mark the memory of those who fell. [416] Former Labour City Councillor Geoff Bridson said 'It's like a secret episode from the past.' [417] On the 10th December 2007 the Lord Mayor of Manchester Councillor Glynn Evans unveiled a new plaque to mark the Peterloo Massacre. The new plaque replaced the existing one at the former Free Trade Hall on Peter Street now the Radisson Edwardian Hotel. [418] The new red plaque is more explicit stating 'St. Peter's Field The Peterloo Massacre, on 16th August 1819 a peaceful rally of 60,000 pro-democracy reformers, men, women and children, was attacked by armed cavalry resulting in 15 deaths and over 600 injuries.' [419] Whilst on 16th August, 2008 a group assembled outside the Radison Edwardian Hotel to mark the 189th anniversary of Peterloo. [420] This year of course, marks the 190th anniversary of the Peterloo Massacre.

[414] Philip Hulme, 'A New Memorial for Peterloo,' *Manchester Forum*, Spring, (2008), p. 7.

[415] *The Guardian*, 13th August, 2007. p. 9.

[416] *Manchester Evening News*, 17th August, 2007.

[417] *Manchester Guardian*, 13th August, 2007. p. 9.

[418] *Manchester City Council News*, 10th December, 2007.

[419] Hulme, *op. cit.*, p. 7.

[420] *South Manchester Reporter*, 7th August, 2008. p. 13.

Dreadful Scene at Manchester Meeting...Anonymous etching
published by J. Evans, London, 27th August 1819.
Manchester Library and Information Service: Manchester Archives and Local Studies

Chapter Four

The Historiography of Peterloo

It is part of a *Left-wing dogma* that Peterloo was an act of
class war perpetrated by Lord Liverpool's government on
the working class, that the 60,000 people peaceably
assembled in St Peter's Field on 16th August 1819 to listen
to Hunt's speech on reform were unprovokedly dispersed
by drunken cavalry who savagely sabred several innocent
people to death and wounded many others, all on the orders
of the panic-stricken specially formed select committee of
magistrates. It needed a Mancunian antiquarian bookseller
of today, Mr. Robert Warmsley, to put the factual record
straight 150 years after the event and after thirty years of
patient and scrupulous research for his monumental book,
Peterloo: The Case Re-opened. [Michael Kennedy] [421]

Although it became known as the Peterloo Massacre, the events
in and around St. Peter's Field on 16th August 1819 were
regarded by both sides with a great deal of passion. At the time
the Peterloo massacre divided English society as a whole, with
petitions and mass meetings being organised *for* and *against* the
position taken by the authorities.[422] As Philip Lawson
emphasises contention lies at the heart of Peterloo because 'one
side argues that the reformers went too far in their protest or
demonstration at St Peter's Field and that in the aftermath of
Peterloo, support for the established order was reaffirmed by the
mass of the population' and 'on the other side exists the view

---

[421]Michael Kennedy, *Portrait of Manchester*, (The Portrait Series), London, (1970), p. 66.
[422] W. A. Speck, *A Concise History of Britain 1707-1975*, Cambridge, (1995), p. 67.

that a legitimate movement of popular constitutionalism ended in a massacre, betrayed on all sides by middle-class equivocation and a corrupt and repressive political system.' [423]

In the aftermath of Peterloo an examination of the historiography shows that Peterloo quickly grew into a battle between the loyalist authorities on the one side and the reformers on the other. [424] In the words of the radical *Manchester Observer*, Peterloo was 'a day of paramount importance to the liberties of our country,' and as 'Big with the fate of Freedom and of Albion.' In contrast, the Reverend Mr Hay thought that; 'The meeting was looked upon, on both sides, as an experiment-a touchstone of the spirit of the Magistrates, and of courage of the mob.' [425]

Within two weeks after Peterloo Francis Philips, a cotton manufacturer and a prominent member of the Pitt Club and Tory party, published *An Exposure of the Calumnies circulated by the Enemies of Social Order and reiterated by their abettors Against the Magistrates and Yeomanry Cavalry of Manchester and Salford,* (1819) defending the behaviour of the Manchester Magistrates and the yeomanry cavalry on the day. This prompted John Edward Taylor to write his riposte *Notes and Observations Critical Explanatory, on the Papers Relative to the Internal State of the Country recently presented in Parliament; To which is intended a Reply to Mr Francis Philip's Exposure,* London, (1820). Meanwhile the Radical press continued to report on protest meetings and trials in an attempt to have the

---

[423] Philip Lawson, 'Reassessing Peterloo,' *'History Today*, March, (1988), pp. 24-25.
[424] Philip Lawson, 'Peterloo: A Constables Eye-View Re-assesed,' *Manchester Regional History Review*, Vol. iii, (1989), p. 39.
[425] Diana Donald, 'The Power of Print: Graphic Images of Peterloo,' *Manchester Regional History Review*, Vol. iii, (1989), p. 21.

aggressors identified and punished without success. In contrast the Tory newspapers continued to make excuses for the Manchester magistrates and the yeomanry cavalry praising them and the military for their conduct.[426]

I would agree with Neville Kirk's analysis that since the late 1950s the historiography of Peterloo has been dominated by three conflicting interpretations.[427] The first interpretation by Donald Read, *Peterloo The 'Massacre' and its Background*, (1957), identifies Peterloo as a massacre although he qualifies this in the preface to his book:

> The successful designation of Peterloo as a 'massacre' represents another piece of successful propaganda. Perhaps only in peace-loving England could a death-roll of only eleven persons have been so described.[428]

Read argues that the 'massacre' was the result of panic and a serious lack of foresight on part of the Manchester magistrates rather from central government direction or premeditation. Read also argues that blame for the deaths and injuries at the August 16th meeting lies with the magistrates but not with the Home Secretary, Lord Sidmouth, who advised the magistrates to use caution and only to use force as a last resort.[429] According to Read:

---

[426]Turner, *op. cit.*, pp. 266-268.
[427] Neville Kirk, 'Commonsense, Commitment And Objectivity: Themes in The Recent Historiography of Peterloo,' *Manchester Regional History Review*, Vol. iii, (1989), p. 61.
[428] Read, *op. cit.*, p. vii.
[429] Kirk, *op. cit.*, p. 61.

The evidence of the Home Office papers was used to show how Lord Sidmouth, the Home Secretary, had advised the Manchester magistrates to act with very great circumspection at the meeting, to collect evidence of any seditious intention, but not to intervene unless violence broke out.[430]

Read's final conclusion is that the central government was not responsible for the massacre. Instead Read argues:

Ominously, on August 3rd the 'loyalist' *Manchester Mercury* newspaper, reported that the Cheshire magistrates had 'come to a determination to act with decision, and to *suppress all Seditious Meetings immediately as they assemble.*' It was this policy, not the one advocated by the Home Office, which produced the Peterloo Massacre. [431]

Read also argues 'How far the attitude of the Home Office differed from that of the Manchester magistrates responsible for the Peterloo massacre was shown in a letter written by Hobhouse to James Norris one of the Select Committee of Magistrates twelve days before Peterloo.' Henry Hobhouse was the under-secretary to the Home Office and urged the magistrates simply to gather evidence of what took place at the meeting to ignore any illegal proceeding for the time being and not to use force. Read produces the following letter as evidence in support of his claim:

---

[430] Read, *op. cit.*, p. 207.
[431] *Ibid*, p. 122.

Lord Sidmouth has no doubt that you will make arrangements for obtaining evidence of what passes; that if anything illegal is done or said, it may be the subject of prosecution. But even if they should utter sedition or proceed to the election of a representative, Lord Sidmouth is of the opinion that it will be the wisest course to abstain from any endeavour to disperse the mob, unless they should proceed to acts of felony or riot...His Lordship [concluded Hobhouse in a similar letter to a Rochdale magistrate eight days later] considers that on various Accounts this mode of proceeding is far preferable to an attempt to disperse the Assembly by force.[432]

Read also stresses 'as the evidence of the Home Office shows, it was never desired or precipitated by the Liverpool Ministry as a bloody repressive gesture for keeping down the lower orders. If the Manchester magistrates had followed the spirit of Home Office Policy there would never have been a massacre.' [433]
The second interpretation by E. P. Thompson in *The Making of The English Working Class*, (1963) argues that:

We shall probably never be able to determine with certainty whether or not Liverpool and Sidmouth were parties to the decision to disperse the meeting by force.[434]

Thompson is critical of Read's book and a highly charged historical debate followed after Thompson writes:

---

[432] *Ibid*, p. 120. Citing, Hobhouse to Norris, 30th June 1819, ; Hobhouse to Crossley, 10th August 1819, (H.O. 41/4).
[433] *Ibid*, p. 207.
[434] Thompson, *op. cit.*, pp. 749-50. *Working Class*

Dr. Read succeeds in writing an entire book on Peterloo without finding space for a single eye witness account by a member of the crowd...It is difficult to follow the argument that an historical technique which screens all the evidence, accepting O.K. witnesses and official papers but rejecting the evidence of people who were ridden down or sabred, is likely to turn out 'scientific' or 'objective' work.[435]

Thompson goes one step further and writes:

There is reason enough to suppose that the Government had determined upon a show-down with the reformers before Peterloo. At some point Old Corruption, faced by swelling demonstrations, a full-blooded Radical press, the election of national representatives, drilling...and threats to withhold taxes, together with ominous symptoms of a growing middle and working-class alliance, was bound either to retreat...or to resort to repression.[436]

It can be seen how these two historical interpretations vary. Donald Read argues that Peterloo was the unfortunate consequence of the lack of foresight on the part of the Manchester magistrates. Whilst E.P. Thompson suspects that it may have been 'planned as a show-down with the radicals' definitely in the case of the magistrates and possibly involving Lord Liverpool's government. Nevertheless, both Read and

---

[435] E. P. Thompson, 'God and King and Law,' *New Reasoner*, 3, (1957-8), p. 79.
[436] *Ibid*, p. 81.

Thompson agree that the evidence suggests that the crowd at Peterloo were 'orderly and generally peaceful.' [437]

The third interpretation by Robert Warmsley in his book *Peterloo: the Case Reopened*, (1969), disagrees with Thompson on practically every issue and with Read in one issue in particular. Warmsley says that 'No one has ever seriously tried to refute the radical interpretation of Peterloo,' and that he intends 'to put the record straight.' Firstly, Warmsley agrees with Donald Read that the central government was not responsible for Peterloo. Secondly, Warmsley attempts to absolve William Hulton the magistrates and the yeomanry from any blame at the Peterloo meeting. He also disagrees with both Read and E. P. Thompson along with the majority of other historians of Peterloo. In fact Warmsley's assertions are nothing more than an endorsement of the testimony given by William Hulton, members of the yeomanry cavalry and special constables. Warmsley's argument is that the yeomanry rode into the crowd not to injure and kill but to arrest Hunt, and that, only when assailed by missiles from a minority of the crowd, did the yeomanry react in self defence. William Hulton, upon seeing the yeomanry under attack, ordered the 15th Hussars to disperse the crowd.[438] Warmsley concludes:

> All the actors in the tragedy were victims. The radicals on the platform, the militants in the crowd, the peaceable in the crowd, the Yeomanry, the constables, the magistrates in their room, and the captives in the New Bayley, were each and severally as much the victims of the tragic chain

---

[437] Kirk, *op. cit.*, pp. 61-66.
[438] *Ibid*, p. 64.

of circumstances as the dead special constable lying in the Bull's Head, the wounded in the infirmary, and Mrs Partington, crushed to death, lying at the bottom of the cellar steps. The *Statesman* sardonically wrote of a Victory; there were no victors and no vanquished, only victims.[439]

The 150th anniversary of Peterloo witnessed the appearance of Jane Marlow's *The Peterloo Massacre*, (1969), a valuable contribution and general reader on this controversial historical topic.[440] At the same time Warmsley's book received some complimentary press, when Michael Kennedy a journalist from the *Daily Telegraph* in his article 'What really happened at Peterloo?' wrote 'Warmsley's massive research challenges the accepted version,' his book 'leaves no fact unchallenged and uncorroborated, no document unread in full, no source unchecked,' and that it 'utterly discredits the accounts in Prentice and Bamford,' furthermore 'In the melee the crowd fled. It seems that most of the casualties were caused by panic and that several people were trampled to death by their fellows.'
[441] This was followed by Michael Kennedy's book *Portrait of Manchester*, London, (1970), in which he also endorses Warmsley's view and asserts:

It is part of a *Left-wing dogma* that Peterloo was an act of class war perpetrated by Lord Liverpool's government on the working class, that the 60,000 people peaceably assembled in St Peter's Field on 16th August 1819 to listen

---

[439] Warmsley, *op. cit.*, p. 233.
[440] *Birkhamstead Gazette*, 8th August, 1969.
[441] *Daily Telegraph*, 16th August, 1969.

to Hunt's speech on reform were unprovokedly dispersed by drunken cavalry who savagely sabred several innocent people to death and wounded many others, all on the orders of the panic-stricken specially formed select committee of magistrates. It needed a Mancunian antiquarian bookseller of today, Mr. Robert Warmsley, to put the factual record straight 150 years after the event and after thirty years of patient and scrupulous research for his monumental book, *Peterloo: The Case Re-opened.*[442]

In addition Michael Kennedy writes:

Why is Peterloo, a comparatively *trivial affair* not to be compared with the riots in Bristol and Nottingham...the facts of Peterloo and the motives behind it are a good deal less lurid than Socialist propaganda has made out over the years...It was an inspired journalist on the staff of the *Manchester Observer*, who, with Waterloo but four years in the past, coined the word Peterloo and by this single idea alone probably ensured that the incidents on St. Peter's Field would have a place in history far beyond their merits or deserts.[443]

Michael Kennedy in defence of the Manchester authorities writes 'before they are condemned utterly as reactionary oppressors let it be remembered that the excesses of the French

---

[442] Kennedy, *op. cit.*, p. 66.
[443] *Ibid*, pp. 68-69.

Revolution were still fresh in the minds of governing authority.'
[444]

In marked contrast on 11th December, 1969, an anonymous review of Robert Warmsley's book appeared in *The Times Literary Supplement*, which was later discovered to be written by E. P. Thompson. This review was later re-published as 'Thompson on Peterloo,' in the *Manchester Regional History Review*, (1989), and later in a series of essays by Thompson in *Making History: Writings on History and Culture*, New York, (1994). In this publication Thompson who argues that:

> Warmsley is mainly interested, in the events of the day of Peterloo, and even more closely in the events of one half-hour of that day-between 1.15 and 1.45 p.m. and yet the fact is that Mr Warmsley has no new facts to adduce about this half-hour at all. Because the main thrust of Mr. Warmsley's argument is that, what happened on the day was unintentional, and the crowd (or part of it) was the first aggressor.' [445]

Thompson also argues that Warmsley 'would have us believe that the Yeomanry were ordered to support the special constables in the execution of the warrant to arrest the speakers and then advanced in reasonable order and without aggressive intention or action into the crowd; and then that the crowd closed in upon them in a menacing manner and the Yeomanry were assailed, at some point close to the hustings, by brickbats and sticks hurled by a portion of the crowd, but that most of the

---

[444] Kennedy, *op. cit.*, p. 63.
[445] Thompson, *op. cit.*, p. 68. *On Peterloo*

Yeomanry kept their heads until Hunt and his fellow speakers had been arrested, and then, increasingly assailed by brickbats and hemmed in on all sides by a threatening crowd they were forced to beat off their attackers only using the flats of their sabres, in self defence.' [446]

Thompson says 'from the outset Warmsley asserts that both Samuel Bamford and Archibald Prentice, 'continued to pass on their own version…as wilful deceivers of posterity' and stresses that:

> Mr. Warmsley became convinced, not only that William Hulton had been unfairly treated by historians, but that he and his fellow magistrates were victims of nothing less than a Radical conspiracy to falsify the events of the day-a conspiracy fostered by Hunt, Bamford and Richard Carlile, and furthered by Archibald Prentice, (author of *Historical Sketches of Manchester*), and John Edward Taylor, of the *Manchester Guardian*, and in which John Tyas, the correspondent of *The Times* who witnessed the events from the hustings, the Rev. Edward Stanley, and dozens of others who were witting or unwitting accessories-a conspiracy so compelling that even Donald Read, in his sober and by no means radical study of *Peterloo* (1957), failed to detect it. [447]

Soon afterwards, Donald Read wrote his contrasting review of 'Peterloo: The Case Re-opened, by Robert Warmsley,' in *History*, Volume, 55, (1970), in which he says:

---

[446] *Ibid*, pp. 68-69.
[447] *Ibid*, pp. 68-69.

It was probably inevitable that a *right wing* reassessment of the responsibility for the Peterloo Massacre would follow the emotional *left wing* interpretation offered by E. P. Thompson in *The Making of the English Working Class.*[448]

Read further points out that both Warmsley and Thompson are dissatisfied with his distribution of responsibility for the massacre in his *Peterloo: the 'Massacre' and its Background,* (1957), although they differ from him for contrasting reasons. Read stresses that Thompson rejected his interpretation arguing that 'Sidmouth was anxious for a violent showdown with the Radicals, and that the absence of evidence for this in the Home Office papers was proof only of Establishment cunning in fixing the record.' Read continues; 'Nevertheless extreme *left-wing* and extreme *right-wing* observers of early Radicalism seem to share a propensity to be deeply impressed by the lack of evidence.' [449]

Further Read argues, 'However, Warmsley dismisses Thompson's argument and agrees with Read that, 'the Home Secretary and his assistants were not responsible for the massacre.' and 'Warmsley is agitated because this inevitably lays responsibility for the tragedy exclusively upon the magistrates, and especially upon their chairman at Peterloo, William Hulton.' Moreover, Read says, 'Warmsley's explicit chief intention is to defend Hulton from what he regards as the calumnies of both contemporaries and historians.' [450]

It can be seen how historical interpretations vary. Firstly Donald Read identifies Peterloo as a massacre, albeit of a

---

[448] Donald Read, 'Peterloo: The Case Re-opened, By Robert Warmsley,' *History,* Vol. 55, (1970), pp. 138-140.
[449] *Ibid.*
[450] *Ibid.*

peculiarly English kind which resulted from panic and serious lack of foresight on part of the Manchester magistrates rather than from central government direction or premeditation. Secondly, E. P. Thompson, sees Peterloo as a bloody class-based massacre in which premeditation was definitely evident in the case of the Manchester magistrates and possibly by Lord Liverpool's government. Thirdly, Robert Warmsley has offered the revisionist argument that Peterloo constituted an unfortunate tragedy rather than a massacre, resulting from a series of mishaps and misunderstandings, and in which there were only victims as opposed to victors and vanquished. [451]

In conclusion the three historical interpretations discussed all have their flaws. Both Read and Warmsley ignore the eye witness accounts and inevitably give a pro *loyalist* bias to their work. On the other hand E. P. Thompson seeks to implicate Lord Liverpool's Government in the massacre without the support of documentary evidence and in the face of the contradictory evidence presented by Donald Read. Other writers have of course, merely repeated one of these interpretations depending on their sympathy or inclination. For example most recently Robert Poole writes 'A conservative strain of history has downplayed Peterloo, which in some versions is relegated to the status of a 'tragedy' or even an 'incident.' [452] In another study the Yeomanry were described as the ''murders of Manchester'' while another reduced all the events of 16th August to ''the St Peter's Field incident.'' [453] As Philip Lawson writes 'the simple fact of interchangeable terms, like incident,

---

[451] Kirk, *op. cit.*, p. 61.
[452] Poole, *op. cit.*, p. 115.
[453] Lawson, *op. cit.*, p. 39. *Peterloo: A Constables Eye-View Re-Assessed*

massacre, demonstration or riot, frequently used as a suffix to Peterloo merely underlines the contention surrounding the issue.'[454] A major problem within the historiography of Peterloo is of course, most historians have not based their research on primary source documentation and eye witness accounts. Instead the history of Peterloo has been largely based on the assumptions of previous writers and their analysis of the facts taken from secondary works which have simply been repeated in every generation. However, I must agree with Robert Poole that 'the contrived debate over 'blame' for the massacre has been unproductive and attempts to exonerate the Manchester authorities have been wholly unconvincing.' [455]

---

[454] Lawson, *op. cit.*, p. 24. *Reassessing Peterloo*
[455] Poole, *op. cit.*, p. 112.

THE RENOWNED

ATCHIEVEMENTS OF PETER-LOO,

ON THE GLORIOUS SIXTEENTH DAY OF AUGUST, 1819.

BY SIR HUGO BURLO FURIOSO DI MULO SPINISSIMO, BART. M. Y. C. and A. S. S.

The Music composed by the celebrated Dr. Horsefood; to be had at the Cat and Bagpipes, St. Mary's-Gate, Manchester.

RECITATIVO.

WHEN fell sedition's stalking through the land,,
It then behoves each patriotic band
Of Noble Minded Yeomen Cavaliers;
To sally forth and rush upon the mob,
And execute the Magisterial Job,
Of cutting off the Ragamuffin's ears.

ARIA BRAVURA.

(Forte.) How valiantly we met that crew
Of infants, men and women too,
Upon the Plain of Peterloo,
And gloriously did hack and hew (a)
The d——d reforming gang;
Our swords were sharp you may suppose,
Some lost their ears—some lost a nose,
Our horses trod upon their toes
E're they could run t' escape our blows,
With shrieks the welkin rang.

(Agitato.) So keen were we to rout these swine,
Whole shoals of constables in line,
We gallop'd o'er in stile so fine,
By orders of the Sapient Nine,
First Friends—then Foes—laid flat;
By Richardson's best grinding skill,
Our blades were set with right good will,
That we these Rogues might bleed or kill,
And "give them of Reform their fill,"
And what d'ye think of that?

(Piano.) They swear, for work they're not half paid,
By th' tyrants of the weaving trade,
Who live like Kings (s) by th' toil they've made—
These lies of us are daily said
By this ragg'd hungry swarm.
No reason have they thus to prate,
While we're recourse to'th Parish rate,
We'll send them there for hours to wait
The diff'rence to receive we 'bate
Of wage—and where's the harm?

(Sotto voce.) These tag-rag, bob-tail herds of brutes,
Are not content with wholesome roots, (c)
But think therewith that beef well suits,
Their chops, e'en water for rare fruits,
The lousy growling dogs;
They think forsooth, that they should dine
Like Gentlefolks, and drink their wine
Or guzzle ale, or eat pig's chine,
For game and fish they even whine,
Rank treason 'mongst these hogs!!

(Pianissima-mente) And then those Owls who think, because
They've filch'd the Pow'r to make our laws,
They'll raise their rents thro'th people's maws,
We'll gull by thunders of applause
For doubling th' price of corn.
We'll curse and fight through "thick and thin,"
All those who make a dev'lish din
About dear bread—for there's no sin
In taking thus the great folks in
For th' Rates by'th Land are borne.

(Con Baldanza) With "ell-wide jaws"(n) we'll roar and sing,
We'll bravely fight for Church and King;
Those who no arms with them shall bring,
And may each vile Reformer swing
That we miss cutting down.
To our good things we'll stick like wax,
And throw the laws upon their backs;
These bare-bone herds we'll make our hacks,
Then nobly gobble Tythe and Tax,
And thus support the Crown.

(a) Haw—Destruction by cutting.
"Then to the next his wrathful hand he bends,
"Of whom he makes such havoc and such riew,
"That swarms of damned souls to hell he sends."
Spencer's Fairy Queen, V.i. VIII. 40.

(s) One of whom declared, he only got thirteen hundred pounds per week, or sixty-seven thousand six hundred pounds a year—See reports of Cases at the New Bailey, for 1848.
This income arising out of a Cotton Factory, forms a much greater amount than the whole estate and emoluments of the great Lord Burleigh, Prime Minister, in the days of Queen Elizabeth for his care of the whole nation; and his present Majesty has only the appropriation of sixty thousand pounds a year out of the Civil List.

(c) "Potatoes, not vegetables."—Wright N. B. M. and one of the nine.
(n) "Spreading their ell-wide Lanthorn Jaws abroad."—Peter Pindar.

Loyalist Song Sheet

Chapter Five

Radical and Loyalist Poetry

Prefatory Lines

In Eighteen Hundred and Nineteen I stood
Upon the famous field of Peterloo,-
Where, met to do their country good,
The million were, the harmless and the true,-
Beside the banner, on which was inscribed
Words breathing freedom for trade in corn;
The *Yeomanry*, who had strong drink imbibed,
Dispersed the people with their banners torn:
Many were killed, and others wounded sore;
A Lancer officer became my friend,
Waving his sword o'er th' path I might explore,
And his assistance he did kindly lend.
Forty long years have travelled to the past,
The future brighter unto me beseems;
True liberty shall be man's lot at last,
Or I am troubled with deceiving dreams:
Meanwhile, a simple poets humble pen
May speak to soldiers and to gentlemen;
And, after many years of worldly strife,
I now must thank a soldier for my life.[456]

February 10, 1860.   E. R.

---

[456] Elijah, Ridings, *The Village Muse, Containing The Complete Poetical Works Of Elijah Ridings*, Macclesfield, (1865), p. 8.

Immediately after Peterloo there was a flood of verse from the loyalists on the one side and the Radicals on the other.[457] A selection of some of this verse is presented in this Chapter. Apart from the indignation that came from both sides after Peterloo, that is, the righteous anger of those who were attacked as well as those who were ordered to attack, there is evidence of what might be regarded as the more emotional responses from both sides in the poetry produced and circulated afterwards. The efforts of the Loyalists were jingoistic and triumphant, those of the Radicals closer to the tragedy.

Loyalist Verse

The Answer to Peterloo

On the sixteenth day of August, eighteen hundred and nineteen,
All in the town Manchester the Rebelly Crew were seen,
They call themselves reformers, and by Hunt the traitor true,
To attend a treason meeting on the plains of Peter-Loo.

Those hearers of their patron's call came flocking into town,
Both Male and Female radical, and many a gapeing clown,
Some came without their breakfast, which made their bellies rue;
But got a warm baggin on the plains of Peter-Loo.

---

[457] Marlow, *op. cit.*, p. 173. *Peterloo Massacre*

From Stayley-Bridge they did advance with a band of music
fine,
And brought a cap of liberty from Ashton-under-lyne ;
There was Macclesfield and Stockport lads, and Oldham
roughheads to,
Came to hear the treason sermon preached by Hunt at Peterloo.

About the hour of one o'clock this champion too the chair,
Surrounded by his aid-de-camps, his orders for to hear,
And disperse them through that Rebelly Mob, which around his
  Standard drew ;
But they got their jackets dusted on the plains of Peterloo.

They hoisted up treason caps and flags, as plainly you may see,-
And with local acclamations shouted Hunt and liberty ;
They swore no man should spoil their plan, but well our
Yeoman
  Knew;
They assembled in St James Square, and marched for Peter-Loo.

The Rochdale band of music, with harmony sublime,
Had placed themselves convenient to amuse Hunt's concubine ;
But soon their big drum was broke, all by our Yeomen true ;
They dropped their instruments, and run away from Peter-Loo.

When the Yeomen did advance the mob began to fly,
Some thousands of old hats and clogs behind there did lie ;
They soon pulled down their *Treason Flags*, and numbers of
them flew ;

And Hunt they took a prisoner on the plains of Peter-Loo.

Now Hunt is taken prisoner and sent to Lancaster gaol,
With seven of his foremost men, their sorrows to bewail ;
His mistress sent to hospital her face for to renew,
For she got it closely shaven on the plains of Peter-Loo.

Success attend those warlike men, our Yeoman Volunteers,
And all their Gallant Officers who knows no dread or fears,
Likewise the *Irish Trumpeter*, that loud his trumpet blew,
And took a cap of liberty from them at Peter-Loo.

Now to conclude and make an end, here's health to George our King,
And all those Gallant Yeomanry whose praises I loudly sing ;
May Magistrates and Constables with zeal their duty do ;
And may they prove victorious upon every Peter-Loo.[458]

Most recently Robert Poole in his article *The March to Peterloo: Politics and Festivity in Late Georgian England*, (2006), has drawn our attention to the fact that on the 17th September 1822, *Aston's Manchester Herald* published the following ultra-loyalist verse:

Though enrag'd by the strokes from the radical sticks,
And the thick-flying missiles, the stones and the bricks,
The Soldiers and Yeoman set bounds to their wrath,
And only kept onwards in stern Duty's path!

---

[458] Warmsley, *op. cit.*, p. 131.

And 'tis wonder, no more, in the scene of confusion,
Then found their life's day brought to sudden conclusion;
For though Opposition cried 'Murder!' from hearsay,
The work of dispersion was done quite in mercy.
There were three lost lives-these were trampled to death,
And one, from a sabre wound, yielded his breath.[459]

Radical Verse

Although the poetical responses to Peterloo have not escaped the attention of Peterloo's historians and whilst references to Shelley's *The Mask of Anarchy* frequently appear, very little effort has been made in examining both the signed and unsigned verses which appeared in the majority of the radical newspapers and periodicals in the aftermath of Peterloo. This verse offers us a new perspective on Peterloo because it explains and challenges the conventional accounts. These verses illustrate how the Radical Poets reacted to the killings and wounding which were inflicted on the crowd. In these poems the Radical writers expressed their own reactions to the Peterloo Massacre and attempted to explain what had actually happened and how they felt about it.[460]

Jim Clayson in his article *The Poetry of Peterloo* highlights the fact that the bulk of the Radical verse dealing with the massacre was published over a two-month period between 11th September and 30th October 1819. Over 30 verses appeared in six radical papers namely *The Medusa, The Theological* and *Political Comet, The Briton, The Cap of Liberty* and *The White Hat.*

---

[459] Poole, *op. cit.*, p. 256.
[460] Jim Clayson, 'The Poetry of Peterloo,' *Manchester Regional History Review*, Vol. iii, (1989), p. 31.

Others appeared in various newspapers and publications in London.[461] For example Samuel Bamford's most celebrated poem of Peterloo appeared in the *Manchester Observer* on 7th August 1819:

The Lancashire Hymn

Have we not heard the infant cry,
And marked his mother's tear;
That look, which told us mournfully,
That woe and want were there,
And shall they ever weep again?
And shall their pleadings be in vain,

By the dear blood which Hampden bled
In freedom's noble strife,
By gallant Sydney's gory head,
By all thats dear to life,
They shall not supplicate in vain,
No longer will we wear the chain.[462]

A verse published in the Radical press was *Stanzas Occasioned By Manchester Massacre*, which appeared in the *Black Dwarf* on 25th August 1819. The writer used the pseudonym 'Hibernicus' suggesting a sympathy or affiliation with Ireland.

Stanzas Occasioned by Manchester Massacre

---

[461] *Ibid,* pp. 31-34.
[462] Read, *op. cit.*, p. 37. ; *Manchester Observer,* 7th August, 1819.

Oh, weep not for those who are freed
From bondage as so frightful as ours!
Let tyranny mourn, for the deed,
And howl o'er the prey she devours!

The mask for a century worn,
Has fallen from her visage at last;
Of all its sham attributes shorn,
Her reign of delusion is past.

In native deformity now
Behold her, how shatt'd and weak!
With murder impress'd on her brow,
And cowardice blanching her cheek.

With guilt's gloomy terror bow'd down,
She scowls on the smile of the slave!
She shrinks at the patriot's frown;
She dies in the grasp of the brave.

Then brief be our wail for the dead,
Whose blood has seal'd tyranny's doom;
And the tears that affliction will shed,
Let vengeance, bright flashes illume.

And shame on the passionless thing
Whose soul can now slumber within him!
To slavery still let him cling,
For liberty scorns to win him.

Her manlier spirits arouse
At the summons so frightfully given!
And glory exults in their vows,
While virtue records them in Heaven.

August 21, Hibernicus [463]

In the succeeding weeks after Peterloo *The People* appeared in
William Hone's *The Political House that Jack Built* :

The People

These are THE PEOPLE all tatter'd and torn,
Who curse the day wherein they were born,
On account of Taxation too great to be borne,
And pray for relief, from night to morn,
Who, in vain, Petition in every form,
Who, peaceably Meeting to ask for Reform,
Were sabred by *Yeomanry Cavalry*, who
Were thank'd by The Man, all shaven and shorn,
All cover'd with Orders-and all forlorn;
THE DANDY OF SIXTY, who bows with grace,
And has a *taste* in wigs, collars, cuirasses, and lace;
Who, tricksters, and fools, leaves the State and its treasure,
And when Britain's in tears, sails about at his pleasure;
Who spurn'd from his presencethe Friends of his youth,
And now has not one who will tell him the truth;

---

[463] Clayson, *op. cit.*, p. 34.

Who took his councils, in evil hour,
The Friends to the Reasons of lawless Power,
That back the Public Informer, who
Would put down the Thing, that, in spite of new Acts,
And attempts to restrain it, by Soldiers or Tax,
Will poison the Vermin, that plunder the Wealth,
That lay in the House that Jack built.[464]

A parody surrounding the Prince Regents' speech at the opening of Parliament was published by Hone in *The Man in the Moon* in 1819, read as follows:

But lo!
CONSPIRACY and TREASON are abroad!
Those imps of darkness, gender'd in the wombs
Of spinning-jennies, winding-wheels, and looms,

In Lunashire-
O Lord!
My Lads and G-tl-n, we've much to fear!
Reform, Reform, the swinish rabble cry-
Meaning of course rebellion, blood, and riot-
Audacious rascals! You, my Lords, and I,
Know 'tis their duty to be starved in quiet...[465]

As early as the 28th August 1819 the Radical *Manchester Observer* published the following verse:

---

[464] William Hone, *The Political House that Jack Built*, (fine edition coloured), London, (1819)

[465] Thompson, *op. cit.*, p. 756. William Hone, *The Man in the Moon*, London, 1819.

This is the field of Peter-loo,
These are the poor reformers who met, on the state of
 affairs to debate; in the field of peter-loo.
These are the butchers, blood-thirsty and bold, who cut,
Slash'd and maim'd young, defenceless and old, who
met, on the state of affairs to debate; in the field of
Peter-loo.

This is *Hurly Burly*, a blustering knave, and foe to the
Poor, whom he,d gladly enslave, who led on the
Butchers, blood-thirsty and bold, who cut, slash'd, and
Maim'd young defenceless and old, who met, on the
state of affairs to debate, in the field of Peter-loo.

These are the just-asses, gentle and mild who to keep the
Peace broke it, by lucre beguiled, and sent Hurly Burly,
A blustering knave, a foe to the poor, whom he'd gladly
Enslave, to lead on the butchers, blood-thirsty and bold,
Who cut slash'd and maim'd young, defenceless and
old, who met on the state of affairs to debate; in the
field of Peter-loo.[466]

 This was followed by Samuel Bamford's own composition, *A
Song of Slaughter*, and his last three verses read as follows:

A Song of Slaughter

Ah, behold their sabres gleaming,

---

[466] Marlow, *op. cit.*, p. 173. *Peterloo Massacre*

Never, never known to spare,
See the floods of slaughter streaming!
Hark the cries that rend the air!

Youth and valour nought availed!
Nought availed beauty's prayer!
E'en the lisping infant failed
To arrest the ruin there!

Give the ruffians time to glory!
Theirs is but a waning day;
We have yet another story,
For the pages of history.

Whilst a prisoner in Llchester gaol Henry Hunt helped to circulate Bamford's poem by sending it out with his own weekly addresses to Radical Reformers with the following, 'N.B. This song is the exclusive property of Samuel Bamford, for whose benefit it is published seperatly, price One Penny.' [467]

On 18th September 1819 the *Manchester Observer* published published the following verse:

Manchester Y---Y Valor

Sad sixteenth of August! Accursed be the day;
When thy field, oh, St. Peter! Was crimson'd with gore;
When blue-mantled bullies, in hostile array,

---

[467] *Ibid*, p. 174.

Struck down to earth the defenceless and poor.

Yes, yes! It was valour to gash the unarmed,
To bear down the aged-the cripple-the child;
It was manly to vanquish the female, alarmed,
To mangle her bosom was gentle and mild.

Ye cowardly brutes! May the Lancashire fair,
With merited scorn, your base doings repay;
May they scoff at the coward, whose half-soldier air
Serves this counterfit lion the more to betray.

May the ghosts of the murdered your slumbers infest,
And drops of their blood be found in your wine;
Thus, sinking in heart, and by conscience opprest,
In remorse, and in fear, may you sicken and pine.[468]

On 22nd September 1819 H. Morton's three verses *The Sword King*, also appeared in the *Black Dwarf*:

The Sword King

Who is it that flies from the tumult so fast
Whom the yeomanry bugles are mingling their blast?
The mother who holds her dear child to her breasts,
And screams, as around her expire the oppress'd;
'Oh! Hush thee my darling! Relinquish thy fears,''
My mother! My mother! The sword king is near!

---

[468] Warmsley, *op. cit.*, pp. 263-264.

The sword king with sabre so bloody and bright,
Ah! Shade my young eyes from the horrible sight!''

'Base brat of reform, shall thy cries bar my way,
To the laurels that bloom for the loyal to day?
Shalt thou live to rear banner, white, emerald, or blue?
No! this is are yeomanry's own Waterloo.''
My mother! My mother! And dust thou not hear
What curses the yeomanry shout in thine ear? ''
'Oh! Hush thee my child, let the murders come!
There is vengeance in heaven for the base who strike
  home!'

'A curse on your standards so flaunting and fine,
Surrender or perish!- die rebel-tis mine! ''
'My mother! My mother! oh! hold me now fast,
The sword king and steed will o'ertake us at last! ''
The mother she trembled,she doubled her speed,
But dark on her path swept the yeoman's black steed;
Life throbb'd in her poor baby's bosom no more.

H. Morton,
Son of Silas Morton [469]

The Bloody Field of Peterloo, appeared in *The Theological And
Political Comet* of 2nd October 1819 and was signed R. S. and
can be attributed to Robert Shorter, who was a printer, publisher

---

[469] Clayson, *op. cit.*, p. 35.

and probably the editor at the time. The last three verses read as follows:

The Bloody Fields of Peterloo

Wives, mothers, children, on the plain,
In one promiscuous heap, I view;
The husband, son, and father slain,
Stetch'd on the field of Peterloo!

But Yeoman's hearts are form'd of steel'
Ardent to fields of blood they go;
Their gallant souls disdain to feel,
Whilst dealing death at Peterloo!

My muse the truth shall ne'er deny;
The good, the wise, the just, we know,
Think you deserve promotion high,
The iron case on Peterloo! [470]

R.S.

The following verse appeared on 20th October 1819, signed J.B., which is another clear demonstration of how some of the working-class were feeling at the time.

Verses For The Boys Of Manchester

---

[470] *Ibid*, p. 35.

Never remember the fifth of November,
Gunpowder treason and plot,
Bloodshed and murder carried much further,
Will make Guy's name forgot.
Blue bloodhounds worse than Guy,

In many a company,
With big wigs
To cut up the people alive.
Unhappy accursed the day,
That saw these monsters go to their prey,
Arm'd cowards on the throng,
Charged with horse and sword along,

The laws we need not fear,
The Doctor keeps all clear,
The swinish people's blood,
Will form the choicest food;
Highest thanks will be our meed,
Then forward 'urge the steed.'

As I was flying over the ground,
I saw the devil with a blue bloodhound,
He grinn'd and look'd like the other,
You'd say he was his own twin brother.
His brains were made of lead,
No shame his heart had fear of,
His valiant hand with a bloody sword,
Cut an old woman's ear off.
A twopenny loaf to feed such an oaf,

A nine tailed cat to hang him,
Exciseable Slop, ne shan't have a drop.
But a good strong drop to hang him.
Hollo boys! Hollo boys! God save the king,
Hollo boys, hollo boys! Let the bells ring. [471]

J. B.

Radical propaganda continued throughout 1819. On the 6th November, Allen Davenport a shoemaker poet published his *Saint Ethelston's Day*. This verse mocked both the Reverend Ethelstone himself and his name for reading the Riot Act and the association of the church with the killings and woundings.

Saint Ethelstone's Day

A Manchester Parson, to church and king staunch,
Much fam'd in the pulpit, but more on the bench,
Resolv'd to be sainted without more delay;
And, the SIXTEENTH OF AUGUST was fixed for
The day.

To contrive the best means, all his genius was bent,
How to celebrate such an auspicious event,
When he saw the Reformers, in marching array,
Move on to the field on SAINT ETHELSTONE'S
DAY.''

---

[471] *Ibid*, p. 35.

Then the oath of his office, inform'd him' twas good,
That the vest of a saint should be sprinkl'd with
Blood;
When his Counsellors whisper'd 'Twill be the best
Way,
The Reformers to crush on SAINT
ETHELSTONE'S DAY.''

He took the advice, and, to make all things sure,
Read the riot act o'er, on the step of his door;
When the Yeomanry Butchers all gallop'd away,
To do some great exploit on SAINT
ETHELSTONE'S DAY.

They hack'd off the breasts of the women, and then,
They cut off the ears and noses of men;
In every direction they slaughtered away,
'Till drunken with blood on SAINT
ETHELSTONE'S DAY.

'Cut away, my brave fellows, you see how they faint,
They are BLACKGUARD REFORMERS!''
Exclaimed the new saint:
'Send them to the Devil, my lads, on your way,
And, no doubt, they'll remember SAINT
ETHELSTONE'S DAY.'' [472]

---

[472] *Ibid*, p. 36.

Shelley reacted to news of Peterloo by writing *The Masque of Anarchy* and several radical songs in the hope that it would arouse the British people to active but nonviolent political protest. He belonged to an aristocratic class who took politics seriously. Shelley was mainly concerned with the larger questions arising out of current politics; the relationship between political and moral issues, the ideas of freedom, liberty and the tyranny of law.[473] News of the Peterloo Massacre reached Shelley on 6th September 1819.[474] He was residing in Italy at the time where he wrote *The Mask of Anarchy*. [475]

The Mask of Anarchy

As I lay asleep in Italy
There came a voice from over the Sea,
And with great power it forth led me
To walk in visions of Poesy.

I met murder on the way-
He had a mask like Castlereagh-
Very smooth he looked, but grim;
Seven blood-hounds followed him:

All were fat; and well they might
Be in admirable plight,
For one by one, and two by two,

---

[473] Woodward, *op. cit.*, p. 33.
[474] Marlow, *op. cit.*, p. 174.
[475] Schama, *op. cit.*, p. 134.

He tossed them human hearts to chew
Which from his wide cloak he drew.

Next came Fraud, and he had on,
Like Eldon, an emined gown;
His big tears, for he wept well,
Turned to mill-stones as the fell.

And the little children, who
Round his feet played to and fro,
Thinking every tear a gem,
Had her brains knocked out by them.

Clothes with the Bible, as with light,
And the shadows of the night,
Like Sidmouth, next Hypocris
On a crocodile rode by.

And many more Destructions played
In this ghastly masquerade,
All disguised, even to the eyes,
Like Bishops, lawyers, peers, or spies.

Last came Anarchy: he rode
On a white horse, splashed with blood;
He was pale even to the lips,
Like death in the Apocalypse.

And he wore a kingly crown;

And in his grasp a sceptre shone;
On his brow the mark I saw-
'I am God, and King, and Law! ' [476]

Samuel Bamford's *Lines to a Plotting Parson*, which was originally written in 1820, and directed at the Reverend Hay, a member of the Select Committee of Magistrates at Peterloo is described by Warmsley in *Peterloo: The Case-reopened*, (1969), as 'one of the bitterest, most vituperative pieces of writing in all the Peterloo canon, because it was aimed at an individual.' [477] It appeared in the collected edition of Bamford's verse in 1864:

Lines to a Plotting Parson

Come over the hills out of York Parson Hay
Thy living is goodly, thy mansion is gay,
Thy flock will be scattered if longer thou stay,
Our Sheperd, our Vicar, the good Parson Hay.

O fear not, for thou shalt have plenty indeed,
Far more than a shepherd so humble will need;
Thy wage shall be ample, two thousand or more,
Which tithes and exactions will bring to thy store.

And here, like a good *loyal* priest thou shalt reign,
The cause of thy patrons with zeal to maintain.
And the poor and hungary shall faint at thy word,

---

[476] Howard Martin, *Britain in The 19th Century*, Cheltenham, (1996), p. 24.
[477] Warmsley, *op. cit.*, p. 132.

As thou doomst them to hell in the name of the Lord.

And here is a Barrack with soldiers enow,
The deed which thou willest all ready to do;
They will rush on the people in martial array,
If thou but thy blood-dripping cassock display.

And Meagher shall ever be close by thy side,
With a brave troop of Yeomanry ready to ride;
For the steed shall be saddled, the sword shall be bare,
And there shall be none the defenceless to spare.

Then the joys that thou felt upon St. Peter's Field,
Each week or each month some new outrage shall yield,
And thy eye which is failing shall brighten again,
And pitiless gaze on the wounded and slain.

Then thy Prince too shall thank thee, and add to thy wealth,
Thou shall preach down sedition and pray for his health;
And Sidmouth, and Canning, and sweet Castlereagh,
Shall write pleasant letters to dear Cousin Hay.

Each dungeon now silent shall sound with a groan,
For the captive shall mourn in its darkness alone;
And the chain shall be polish'd which now hangs in rust,
And brighten'd the bar which is mouldering to dust. [478]

---

[478] *Ibid*, pp. 132-133.

Two verses *The Meeting at Peterloo* and *Manchester Meeting, A New Song*, have been presented by Joyce Marlow in her article 'The Day of Peterloo':

The Meeting at Peterloo

Come lend an ear of pity while I my tale do tell,
It happened at Manchester a place that's known right well,
For to redress our wants and woes reformers took their way,
A lawful Meeting being called upon a certain day.
So God bless Hunt, &C.

The Sixteenth day of August Eighteen hundred and
Nineteen.
There many thousand people on every road were seen,
From Stockport, Oldham, Ashton & other places too,
It was the largest Meeting Reformers ever knew.

Brave Hunt was appointed that day to take the chair.
At one o'clock he did arrive our shouts did rend the air,
Some females fair in white and Green near the hustings
Stood,
And little did we all expect to see such scenes of blood,
Scarcely had Hunt began to speak three cheers was all
The cry,
What to shout for we little knew but still we did comply,
He saw the enemies surround be firm said he my friends
But little still we did expect what would be their ends
Our enemies so cruel regardless of our woes,

They did agree to force us from the Plain of Peterloo,
But if that we had been prepared or any cause for fear
The regulars might have cleared the ground, and they
Stood in the rear,
Then to the fatal ground they went, and thousands
Tumbled down,
And many armless female lay bleeding on the ground
No time for flight was gave us still every road we fled.
But heaps on heaps were trampled down some wounded
and some dead.

Brave Hunt was then arrested and several others too.
Then marched to the New Bailey, believe me it is true,
Numbers there was wounded and many there was slain,
Which makes the friends of those dear souls so loudly
To come plain.

O God look down upon us for thou art just and true,
And those that can no mercy shew thy vengeance is
their due.
Now quit this hateful mournful scene look forward with
This hope,
That every Murderer in this land may swing upon a rope,
But soon reform shall spread around for sand the tide
Won't stay,
May all the filth that in our land right soon be wash'd
away,
And may sweet harmony from hence in this our land
Be found,

May we be blest with plenty in all the country round. [479]

Manchester Meeting
A New Song

It was in the year one thousand,
Eight hundred and nineteen,
All in the month of August,
Our Weaver lads was seen,
Each bush and tree was in full bloom,
And sun Bright did shine,
To be a glorious witness
For our weaver lads to joint.
Chorus.

Along with Hunt, &c.
From Stockport town and Ashton,
The weaver lads came in,
Who all behav'd with honour bright,
The Meeting to begin,

Upon the ground they all did meet
Like heroes of renown,
Search all the mannor,d nation,
Our match cannot be found.
The weaver lads from Stockport,
Did all come flocking down,
From Oldham and from Middleton,

---

[479] Marlow, *op. cit.*, p. 6.

And all the country round,

Come let us all rejoice and sing,
And hope for better days,
Through Lancashire and Cumberland,
We'll sing the weavers praise.
Then Sir C. Wolsely in Manchester,
Behav'd with honour bright.

Squire Hunt spoke with courage bold,
When he appeared in sight,
With respect unto our weaver lads,
He never meant any ill.
And in bright shining pages,
We'll sing his praises still.

Now here's health to Mr Hunt,
Long may he rule this soil,
And likewise all his gentlemen,
Long may the live and smile,
And let us not forget the day,
That we held up our hands,
We hope to flourish once again,
All in our native land.

Now to conclude and end my song,
I have little more to say,
May our British Manufactures
Flourish more every day,

And our trade shall flourish again,
Through all the British Isles,
Both Lancashire and Cumberland,
And Cheshire likewise.

A Peterloo ballad Innes, Printer, Manchester [480]

The following verse appeared in the *Manchester Observer* on 26th February 1820:

For spies they shall work by the window at night,
Like bloodhounds, to smell out the prey of thy spite;
And laugh shall be hush'd, and the townsmen shall meet,
But none, e'en his neighbour shall venture to greet,

And now, gloomy famine shall stalk thro' the land,
No comfort the poor shall receive at thy hand;
And the window shall curse thee whilst life doth remain,
And the orphan shall lisp back her curses again.

And the night wind shalt sound like a scream in thine ear,
And the tempest shalt shake thee with terrible fear,
And the zephyr, which fans thee, shall bring thee no cure;
It will whisper a tale which thou can'st not endure.

And the day shall arise but its joys will be fled,
And the season of darkness shall add to thy dread;
And a mark of affliction thou ever shalt be,

---

[480] *Ibid*, p. 7.

And none shall partake of thy trouble with thee.

Middleton, January, 12th 1820. B. [481]

The verse *Prefatory Lines* was written by Elijah Ridings who was a radical poet in the post-Napoleonic era and a well known working-class poet of Manchester in early Victorian Britain. His volumes included *The Village Muse* and *The Village Festival* signed copies of his works are located at Chetham's Library in Manchester.   Ridings was in the crowd at Peterloo, and was saved by a regular officer in the army who called out to him, 'Be quick young man ; this way,' and pointing out to him with his sword, a way of escape.' [482] This last poem written 40 years after Peterloo reflects the ideals of a Radical softened by the passage of time. Written in 1860 he is more reflective and philosophical as well as indicating his hope for the future.

Prefatory Lines

In Eighteen Hundred and Nineteen I stood
    Upon the famous field of Peterloo,-
Where, met to do their country good,
    The million were, the harmless and the true,-
Beside the banner, on which was inscribed
    Words breathing freedom for trade in corn;
The *Yeomanry*, who had strong drink imbibed,
    Dispersed the people with their banners torn :
Many were killed, and others wounded sore;

---

[481] Warmsley, *op. cit.*, p. 134.
[482] Swindles, *op. cit.*, p. 187.

A Lancer officer became my friend,
Waving his sword o'er th' path I might explore,
    And his assistance he did kindly lend.
Forty long years have travelled to the past,
    The future brighter unto me beseems;
True liberty shall be man's lot at last,
 Or I am troubled with deceiving dreams:
Meanwhile, a simple poets humble pen
May speak to soldiers and to gentlemen;
And, after many years of worldly strife,
I now must thank a soldier for my life.[483]

February 10, 1860.   E. R.

Angus-Butterworth in his *Lancashire Literary Worthies*, (1980), believes the list of writings by Ridings is impressive. His first publication was *Poetical Works* (1848), followed by *The Village Festival*, (1848), and two years later *Pictures of Life*, (1850). Although his own dialect writings were few, he later edited *The Lancashire Muse*, (1853). A more ambitious venture was made by Ridings with his *The Village Muse*, (1854), containing the 'Complete Poetical Works of Elijah Ridings,' which included a biographical sketch of him. This was followed by *The Poets Dream*, (1856); and *The Volunteers*, (1860), which he described as 'A Ryme of Commerce and Liberty.' After Ridings turned 60 he returned to his original work with *Streams from an Old Fountain*, (1863), which proved to be the last of his

---

[483] Ridings, *op. cit.*, p. 8.

books. He died in Manchester on 18th October 1872 and was buried in Harpurhey Cemetery.[484]

In conclusion it has been demonstrated in this Chapter that Loyalist verse was jingoistic and triumphant and Radical verse was closer to the tragedy. I would agree with the analysis of Jim Clayson who believes that 'looking at the working-class response to Peterloo through the popular literature it created gives us a new perspective on events. The radicals were concerned less with constitutional issues, they presupposed the meeting was legal, than with the behaviour of the new middle-classes. They perceived them to have formed an alliance with aristocratic government.' [485]

---

[484] L.M. Angus-Butterworth, *Lancashire Literary Worthies*, St. Andrews, (1980), pp. 123-4.

[485] Clayson, *op. cit.*, p. 37.

Chapter Six

Concluding Peterloo

Throughout this book I have used the relevant historiography and selected contemporary sources, to illustrate the diversity of opinion about Peterloo and to suggest that many of the myths associated with this event are of questionable historical validity, or, that at least, there are other more plausible well documented interpretations and eyewitness accounts that warrant equal consideration.

In 1819 Manchester was only one of several industrial centres where unenfranchised working men had organised themselves into clubs to discuss political topics, to make plans for a constitutional reform of Parliament and to hasten this reform by means of demonstrations which were intended to persuade the ruling class. The industrial towns in Lancashire looked to Manchester to take the lead. Here the reform movement was more vigorous but was also more carefully watched by the local magistrates.[486]

In 1815, the ruling classes in Britain were still convinced that only they were fit to rule and their interests were those of society as a whole. Therefore when Britain entered the economic crisis after the close of the Napoleonic War in 1815, the aristocratic rulers of Britain concentrated on protecting their own *property* and repressing all threats to their position of power and authority. There is no doubt that the Government and the ruling classes still believed in the possibility of a popular revolution similar to the savage French revolution that had taken place

---

[486] H. W. C. Davis, *Lancashire Reformers, 1816-1817*, London, (1926), Reprinted from 'The Bulletin of the John Rylands Library,' Vol. 10, No. I, January, (1926)

twenty years earlier. Their official reaction was to repress all agitation rather than to deal with the causes of it.[487]

By 1815 the parliamentary system in Britain had almost gone back to the Middle Ages, certainly not reflecting the needs of the rapidly changing society. Altogether there were '658 MPs in the House of Commons' but how they were elected was to come under close scrutiny. This is largely because there were no independent MPs representing the new expanding industrial centres like Manchester and her surrounding towns.[488] The working classes blamed their misery on misgovernment and the fact that they had no proper representation in parliament to redress their grievances. They could see Manchester, Salford, Bolton, Blackburn, Rochdale, Bury, Ashton-under-Lyne, Oldham, and Stockport had no members, whilst a host of small villages with only a few inhabitants often had two MPs.[489]

As we have seen by 1819, deference had been considerably weakened in whole regions of England by Dissent, Methodism and also challenged by Luddism the Hampden Clubs and the Union Societies.[490] In addition Radical activity in Lancashire in 1819 was particularly strong. This was due to a Radical Press, Radical mass meetings, Radical schools and societies and of course the Radical programme itself. This largely explains although it does not justify the fear and panic of the local authorities at Peterloo. On the one hand the Manchester magistrates were more concerned with what was happening in Lancashire, whilst on the other Lord Sidmouth and the government at Westminster could see a pattern of Radical

---

[487] Evans and Pledger, *op. cit.*, p. 8.
[488] Strong, *op. cit.*, p. 387.
[489] Prentice, *op. cit.*, p. 146.
[490] Thompson, *op. cit.*, p. 737.

activity emerging throughout the country. Therefore by 1819 the Radical background to Peterloo can only be described as being nation-wide.[491]

It was demonstrated in Chapter One that the policy in Regency England was to call on the regular army in troubled times to act as a police force [492] but the main representatives of law and order were the local magistrates, many of whom, like the Manchester magistrates, belonged to an elite oligarchy having little sympathy with the working-class or even with the new smaller mill owners. Their main anxiety was that there would be an assault on property by the mob. Because there was no organised police force, they often swore-in special constables or asked the Home Secretary Lord Sidmouth to authorise the use of the regular army.[493] There is no doubt that this policy was adopted by the Manchester authorities before the Radical reform meeting held on 16th August 1819. In fact preparations by the Manchester authorities were very similar to those made the day before the Blanketeers meeting held in St Peter's Field in 1817.[494]

During the summer of 1819 there occurred a mass mobilization of popular support for political reform.[495] This was reflected by the fact that the weeks leading up to Peterloo witnessed lots of small meetings followed by more impressive demonstrations in regional centres like Manchester, in June and in Birmingham, Leeds and London in July.[496] In addition there had been a

---

[491] Read, *op. cit.*, p. 56.

[492] White, *op. cit.*, p. 190-91.

[493] Asa Briggs, *The Age of Improvement 1783-1876*, London, (1979), p. 213.

[494] Davis, *op. cit.*, p. 32.

[495] *Ibid*, p. 61.

[496] Thompson, *op. cit.*, p. 749.

number of reform meetings held in various parts of Lancashire over the previous, two months. These meetings took place at Oldham, Ashton and Stockport in June, followed by Blackburn, Rochdale, Macclesfield, in July, and Leigh in early August. These meetings were a clear demonstration of the extent of popular support which the Radical Reform Movement enjoyed. It also showed how well the movement was organised, with Reform Unions drawing massive crowds much to the alarm of the Manchester authorities.[497]

There seems little doubt that the Radical reformers on the one hand and the Loyalists on the other expected some form of confrontation to tip the balance in their favour.[498] Therefore, it is not surprising that the animosity between them was becoming very intense.[499] It was against this background that the mood was set for the August meeting which was the climax of a series of political meetings held in Manchester, and its surrounding districts in 1819, a year of industrial depression and high food prices. The organisers intended that a mass meeting would be a great peaceful demonstration of discontent and its political purpose was to put pressure on the Central Government to bring about parliamentary reform.[500] In the words of Donald Read:

> There can be no doubt that the condemnation of William Hulton and the Special Select Committee of Magistrates is justified. Nobody can deny what the mass meeting was all about. The radical protesters were carrying banners demanding-Universal Suffrage, No Boroughmongering,

[497] Bush, *op. cit.*, p. 38.
[498] Turner, *op. cit.*, p. 262.
[499] Turner, *op. cit.*, p. 117. *British politics in an age of reform*
[500] Kidd, *op. cit.*, p. 87.

and No Corn Laws. Hulton and the Regency Tories refused the masses their political rights, and also expected many of them to acquiesce in near *starvation* caused by the deep post-war economic depression.[501]

In Chapter Two it was demonstrated that a massive crowd attended the reform meeting in St Peter's Field including a high proportion of women and children. None of them were armed and their conduct was peaceable. The Select Committee of Magistrates who were obviously nervous before the meeting and alarmed at the size and discipline of the crowd so they ordered the Manchester Yeomanry to arrest the speakers on the Hustings immediately after the meeting began. The fact that the Manchester Yeomanry were the first on the field was the last link in the chain of events leading up to the Peterloo massacre. These men were ardent in their politics, and had suffered from the taunts of the Radicals. There was also a feeling in the air that they were not likely to show much moderation in a crisis. In addition their prejudices had been further aggravated by the fact that during the morning of the 16th, 'while gathering in the taverns to have their boots cleaned and their horses curried, [currie combed] they had become half-drunk.' [502] The unrestrained Manchester Yeomanry did not then confine themselves to seizing the speakers, but instead, wielding their sabres, made a deliberate and general attack on the crowd. William Hulton, the Chairman of the Select Committee of Magistrates, then ordered the 15th Hussars and the Cheshire

---

[501] Donald Read, Review of 'Peteterloo: The Case Reopened by Robert Warmsley,' *History*, Vol., 55, (1970), pp. 138-140.
[502] Read, *op. cit.*, p. 133, citing *The Whole Proceedings before the Coroner's Inquest at Oldham, on the body of John Lees*, J. A. Dowling, (ed.), (1820), p. 459.

Yeomanry to rescue the Yeomanry and disperse the defenceless crowd.[503] Reports indicate that within the space of 10 minutes St Peter's Field was cleared except for the bodies of the dead and injured.[504]

The popular belief that there had been no premeditation by the Select Committee of Magistrates to disperse the meeting by force and that the magistrates were only guilty of incompetence or ill-judgement and everything happened by chance [505] is contradicted by the evidence. In fact two days before the meeting the Reverend Mr Hay stated that magistrates were satisfied that the meeting 'if assembled as it was expected, would be an illegal Meeting.' [506] Therefore, although the magistrates had no power to prohibit the meeting beforehand, they assumed that it would turn out to be illegal and made plans to disperse it by the use of civil and military force.[507] The forces were assembled and warrants were issued to arrest the speakers before the meeting began. The popular belief that is developed in the historiography that most of the injuries were caused by the fleeing crowd crushing one another is simply a myth. Evidence was presented in Chapter Two has shown that most of the injuries were caused by the use of sabres and truncheons and the use of cavalry rather than by the crowd itself. The belief that the 15th Hussars only used the flats of their swords is equally fanciful. Evidence has shown that although the Hussars showed more restraint than the Yeomanry, with the majority using the flats of their swords to disperse the crowd, a small number used

---

[503] Redford, *op. cit.*, p. 254.
[504] *Bamford Passages*, I, *op. cit.*, p. 208.
[505] Stevenson, *op. cit.*, p. 284.
[506] Hay to Simouth, 7th October, 1819, in Thompson, *op. cit.*, p. 74. *On Peterloo*
[507] Redford, *op. cit.*, p. 252.

the cutting edges which inflicted serious wounds. In the same way the belief that only 11 people were killed and 400 injured has been disproved by recent research that has established that there were 'at least 654 casualties, 18 of who died of their injuries.' [508] Finally, the belief that Manchester's Irish population did not become integrated into the movement for parliamentary reform is also unfounded. Research has shown that at least '97 of the injuries recorded in the casualty lists of Peterloo were to persons of Irish extraction, either immigrants from Ireland or those born in England of Irish parents.' [509]

Finally, in concluding Chapter Two it was shown that on 16th August 1819 a massive crowd had gathered in St Peter's Field peacefully and carrying no weapons to put pressure on the government to bring about parliamentary reform. In spite of these factors and, on the orders of the Select Committee of Magistrates were 'attacked by soldiers with sabres and bayonets, and by police with truncheons and staves.' This latest historical research has revealed that there is no doubt that these injuries were inflicted by the authorities quite deliberately. The fact that the military and police attacked an unarmed crowd of civilians, including women and children, both in St Peter's Field and in the streets surrounding it, goes to show that their real intention was to teach these people a terrifying and unforgettable lesson.[510]

In Chapter Three it was demonstrated that although it became known as the Peterloo Massacre, the events in and around St. Peter's Field on 16th August 1819 were regarded by both sides

---

[508] Bush, *Preface*.
[509] *Ibid.*
[510] *Ibid*, p. 52.

with a great deal of passion. The reformers were regarded with fear and suspicion by the establishment, and treated accordingly. This treatment resulted in further agitation which in turn led to increased repressive government reaction. When it came to the question of public order, the Government and the local authorities were ferocious in suppressing discontent, as the story of Peterloo illustrates. The first reaction of the Government to Peterloo was further repression, and the famous Six Acts were passed soon after Peterloo. They were intended to prevent large public meetings, suppress the radical press, and undermine the whole movement for radical reforms.[511] Nevertheless, Peterloo was a turning point in British history. This was largely because the working-class gained a lot of middle-class sympathy.[512]

In Chapter Four and throughout this book it was shown how *right* wing and *left* wing interpretations vary. Another major problem within the historiography of Peterloo is of course, most historians have not based their research on primary source documentation and eye witness accounts. Instead the history of Peterloo has been largely based on the assumptions of previous writers and their analysis of the facts taken from secondary works and simply been repeated in every generation. However, I must agree with Robert Poole that 'the contrived debate over 'blame' for the massacre has been unproductive and attempts to exonerate the Manchester authorities have been wholly unconvincing.' [513] Nevertheless, although the Manchester magistrates had initiated the policy of repression at Peterloo Lord Liverpool's' Government endorsed it with every means at

---

[511] David Thomson, *England in the Nineteenth Century 1815-1914*, Harmondsworth, (1979), p.40.

[512] Aspin, *op. cit.*, p. 61.

[513] Poole, *op. cit.*, p. 112.

its disposal. For example Henry Hunt, John Cartwright, Sir Francis Burdett, Richard Carlile, Sir Charles Wolsley and James Wroe of the *Manchester Observer* were only a few of those imprisoned or awaiting prosecution by the end of 1819.[514]

Chapter Five demonstrates that Loyalist verse was jingoistic and triumphant and Radical verse was closer to the tragedy. In the words of Jim Clayson 'looking at the working-class response to Peterloo through the popular literature it created gives us a new perspective on events. The radicals were concerned less with constitutional issues, they presupposed the meeting was legal, than with the behaviour of the new middle-classes. They perceived them to have formed an alliance with aristocratic government.' [515]

In conclusion the Peterloo Massacre was the result of over-reaction by the Manchester authorities at what otherwise was likely to have been a peaceful demonstration. The brutal dispersal by cavalry on orders from the Manchester authorities of the Radical reform meeting in St Peter's Field on 16th August 1819 bears witness to the profound fears of the privileged-classes in the years following the Napoleonic Wars. [516] Nevertheless, Peterloo was a major turning point in British history. This was largely because the working-class gained a great deal of middle-class sympathy and support for their cause helped greatly by Shelley's *The Mask of Anarchy*, and although the Government passed the notorious Six Acts to end all agitation it did not succeed and eventually came to see that government repression of a disenfranchised people would never

---

[514]Thompson, *op. cit.*, p. 750. *Working Class.*
[515] Clayson, *op. cit.*, p. 37.
[516] Marshall, *op. cit.*, p. 159.

work.[517] For the working-classes, Peterloo came to symbolize the privileged high and mighty tyrannical Tory. Even today 'Peterloo is a forcible and enduring reminder of the power of class in modern British society.' [518]

---

[517] Aspin, *op. cit.*, p. 61.
[518] Kirk, *op. cit.*, p. 66.

Archibald Prentice
Manchester Library and Information Service: Manchester Archives and Local Studies

Appendix

Obituary Notice, Manchester Guardian 19th October, 1872

Death of Elijah Ridings-This poet and politician in humble life breathed his last yesterday in one of our public institutions, where he was carried a little over a month ago suffering from an injury to his thigh caused by a fall in the street. The chief incidents of his not uneventful life are worth recording. Elijah Ridings was born on the 27th November 1802, at Failsworth, and was consequently in his 70th year at his death. His parents were silk weavers with a family of fifteen children, of whom Elijah was the tenth. He was unable to walk until he was three years old, in consequence of disability of the lower part of the vertebral column. He was removed from school at an early age in order that he might wind bobbins for his brothers and sisters who were employed upon silk looms. Subsequently his family moved to Newton Heath, and he became a teacher in the Sunday school attached to St George's Church, Oldham Road. At a later period he joined the Unitarian Chapel, Dob Lane, Failsworth. He still worked at the loom, but in his leisure read such books as came within reach, more particularly history and travels. In the year 1819, being then 17 years of age, he was appointed leader of a section of parliamentary reformers at Newton Heath and Miles Platting on the memorable march to Peterloo; and he narrowly escaped being trampled by the yeomanry horses at the famous meeting on the 16th August in that year. In 1826 he wrote a poem entitled 'The Swan,' which was published in London, in 'Arliss's Pocket Magazine.' In conjunction with a Mr. John Harper, Ridings originated the Miles Platting Zetitic Society, from which sprung the Miles Platting Mechanics

Institution. In 1829 he became the agent of Messrs Pigot and Company, and assisted in the compilation of the National Commercial Directory. Afterwards he assisted in compiling the Liverpool and Birmingham Directories; but, his health failing him, he returned home, where he published a small collection of poems entitled 'The Village Muse.' Some of the poems were in the Lancashire dialect and of a humorous nature and they became popular. The great petition which was sent from Manchester praying that the Reform Bill might pass into law was drawn up under the management of Mr R. Potter, M.P.; Mr. G. Gill and Elijah Ridings, and the latter was employed to superintend the progress of the petition. To him, also and his relatives and friends is mainly attributed the inclusion of the township of Newton Heath within the borough of Manchester. Later he became a lecturer in English literature, and had also delivered addresses in favour of the repeal of the Corn Laws. He started a day school in Lamb Lane, Collyhurst, but in 1832 a visitation of cholera left him with only ten scholars and the school was closed. In May of that year he married, and took a public house in Butler Street, Manchester, the Falstaff and Bardolph. He kept this house for three years, but the failure of an adjacent chemical works on which he had mainly depended, obliged him to give it up; and he then entered into the book trade, in which he continued till within a short time of the date of the accident which resulted in his death. He had considerable taste and judgement as to rare and curious books, and frequently picked up good things at sales. His shop was in Lower King Street. His poetical works were first published in a small book of 80 pages in 1840. In the year of the first exhibition in Hyde Park he wrote an ode 'The Isles of Britain.' 'The Village Muse' mentioned above, contained all the authors writings up to the year in which the work was published, about 1853, and passed through several editions. Since then he has also written 'The Volunteer,' a rhyme prompted by the citizen soldier movement of twelve years ago; and 'Streams from an Old Fountain,' which saw the light in 1863.[519]

---

[519] *Manchester Guardian*, 19th October, 1872.

Bibliography

Unpublished Sources

Chetham's Library, Manchester

Association for the Preservation of Constitutional Order against Levellers and Republicans, constitution and minutes of committee, (1792-99).
Hay, Reverend W.R. Commonplace Book; and Hay Scrapbooks (uncatalogued).
Pitt Club, Manchester, papers (1812-31).

Contemporary Books and Pamphlets

Carlile, Richard. *The Republican*, No. 1, Vol. 1, 27th August, 1819.
Hone, W. *The Political House that Jack Built*, (fine edition coloured), London, (1819).
Hunt, Henry. *Letters to Radical Reformers*, London, (1822-1823).
Huish, Robert, *The History of the Private Life of the late Henry Hunt, Esq.*, II, (London 1836).
Inquest on the Body of John Lees, the Whole proceedings before the Coroner's Inquest at Oldham on the body of John Lees, who died of sabre wounds at Manchester. Taken in shorthand with a plan of St Peter's Field. Edited by Joseph A. Dowling, London, (1820).
Parliamentary Debates, *Papers Relative to the Internal State of the Country*, XLI, (1820-1823).

Philips, Francis. *Exposure of the Calumnies Circulated by the Enemies of Social Order and reiterated by their abettors Against the Magistrates and Yeomanry Cavalry of Manchester and Salford*, London, (1819).

Reports of State Trials, Vol. 1 New Series Appendix B. (1820-1823).

Taylor, John Edward. Notes *and Observations, Critical and Explanatory, on the Papers Relative to the Internal State of the Country recently presented in Parliament; To which is intended a Reply to Mr Francis Philip's Exposure*, London, (1820).

Wooler, T. J. *The Black Dwarf*, Vol. III, (1819).

Newspapers

Manchester Chronicle, 19th June, 1817.

Manchester Observer, 31st July, 1819.

Manchester Mercury, 3rd August, 1819.

Manchester Observer, 7th August, 1819.

Manchester Observer, 16th August, 1819.

The Star, 17th August, 1819.

Manchester Observer, 17th August, 1819.

Manchester Guardian, 18th August, 1819.

Manchester Guardian, 21st August, 1819.

Manchester Observer, 21st August, 1819.

Manchester Observer, 23rd August, 1819.

The Times, 23rd August, 1819.

The Times, 24th August, 1819.

Manchester Observer, 24th August, 1819.

Manchester Observer, 28th August, 1819.

Manchester Chronicle, 28th August, 1819.

The Times, 3rd September, 1819.

Manchester Observer, 6th September, 1819.

Manchester Observer, 18th September, 1819.

The Times, 27th September, 1819.

Manchester Chronicle, 27th November, 1819.

Manchester Mercury, 30th November, 1819.

Manchester Observer, 22nd January, 1820.

The Manchester Guardian, 19th October, 1872.

Birkhamstead Gazette, 8th August, 1969.

Daily Telegraph, 16th August, 1969.

The Times Literary Supplement, 11th December, 1969.

The Guardian, 13th August, 2007.

Manchester Evening News, 16th August, 2007.

The Guardian, 27th November, 2007.

Manchester Evening News, 19th March, 2008.

South Manchester Reporter, 7th August, 2008.

Secondary Sources

Albrecht, J. *Major Hugh Hornby Birley*, in *Transactions of Lancashire and Cheshire Antiquarian Society*, Vol. XL.(1922-1923), Manchester, (1925).

Alderman, Geoffrey. *Modern Britain 1700-1983*, Groom Helm Ltd, Beckenham, (1986).

Angus-Butterworth, L. M. *Lancashire Literary Works*, Henderson and Sons Ltd, St. Andrews, (1980).

Arrowsmith, Peter. *Stockport A History*, Stockport Metropolitan Borough Council, (1997).

Aspinall, Arthur. *The Early Trade Unions*, The Batchworth Press, London, (1949).

Aspin, Chris. *The First Industrial Society, Lancashire, 1750-1850*, (revised edition) Carnegie Publishing Ltd, Preston, (1995).

Ayerest, David. *Guardian, Bibliography of a Newspaper*, Collins, London, (1971).

Axon, William, E. A. (eds), *Annals Of Manchester, A Chronological Record From The Earliest Times To The End Of 1885*, John Heywood, Manchester, (1886).

Bamford, S. *Passages in the Life of a Radical*, Manchester, (1841).

Bamford, S. *Passages in the Life of a Radical*, Manchester, (1844).

Belchem, John. *Industrialization and the Working Class: The English Experience, 1750-1900*, Scholar Press, Aldershot, (1991).

Black, Jeremy. *George III America's Last King*, Yale University Press, New Haven, (2006).

Briggs, Asa. *Victorian Cities*, Pelican Books, Harmondsworth, (1971).

Briggs, Asa. *The Age of Improvement 1783-1867*, Longman, London, (1979).

Bee, Malcolm. *Industrial Revolution and Social Reform in the Manchester Region*, (second edition), Neil Richardson, Manchester, (1997).

Brindley, W.H. (eds.), *The Soul of Manchester*, Manchester University Press, Manchester, (1929).

Brock, W. R. *Lord Liverpool and Liberal Toryism 1820 to 1827*, Frank Cass & Co. Ltd, London, (1967).

Brooks, Ann and Haworth, Brian. *Boomtown Manchester 1800-1850*, The Portico Library, Manchester, (1993).

Bruton, F.A. *The Story of Peterloo*, Manchester University Press, Manchester, (1919).

Bruton, F.A. *Three Accounts of Peterloo by Eyewitnesses, Bishop Stanley, Lord Hylton, Benjamin Smith*, Manchester University Press, Manchester, (1921).

Bruton, F.A. *Short History of Manchester and Salford*, Sherratt & Hughes, Manchester, (1924).

Bush, Michael. *The Casualties of Peterloo*, Carnegie Publishing Ltd, Lancaster, (2005).

Clark, J.C.D. *English Society 1688-1832*, Cambridge University Press, (1985).

Clark, George, Sir. *English History A Survey*, Oxford University Press, (1978).

Crosby, Alan. *A History of Lancashire*, Phillimore & Co. Ltd, (1998).

Darvall, F.O. *Popular Disturbance and Public Order in Regency England*, Oxford University Press, (1926).

David, Saul. *Prince of Pleasure, The Prince of Wales and the Making of the Regency*, Atlantic Monthly Press, New York, (1998).

Derry, T.K., and Jarman, T.L. *Modern Britain, Life and Work through Two Centuries of Change*, John Murry Publishers Ltd, London, (1979).

Dinwiddy, J.R. *From Luddism to the First Reform Bill: Reform in England 1810-1832*, Basil Blackwell Ltd, Oxford, (1986).

Edwards, Michael M. *The Growth of the British cotton trade 1780-1815*, Manchester University Press, Manchester, (1967).

Evans, Eric J. *The Forging of The Modern State, Ealy Industrial Britain 1783-1870,* Longman Group Limited, London, (2001).

Evans Lloyd, and Pledger, Philip, J. *Triumph and Tribulation, A Political and Social History of Britain Since 1815,* Cheshire Publishing Pty Ltd, Melbourne, (1972).

Fisher, H. A. L. *A History of Europe Volume II: From the Early 18th Century to 1935,* Volume II, Fontana/Collins, Glasgow, (1979).

Frangopulo, N.J. *Tradition in Action The Historical Evolution of the Greater Manchester County,* E.P. Publishing, Wakefield, (1977).

Gash, Norman. *Aristocracy and People, Britain 1815-1865,* Edward Arnold Publishers Ltd, London, (1979).

Gooderson, P. J. *A History of Lancashire,* B. T. Batsford, London, (1980).

Gilbert, Alan, D. *Religion and political stability in early industrial England,* in Patrick O'Brien and Roland Quinault, (ed.), *The Industrial Revolution and British Society,* Cambridge University Press, Cambridge, (1993).

Gregg, Pauline. *A Social and Economic History of Britain 1760-1972,* Harrap, London, (1973).

Harland, John. *Ballads and Songs of Lancashire,* (second edition), George Routledge and Sons, (1875).

Hewitt, Eric, J. *A History of Policing in Manchester,* E. J. Morten Publishers, Manchester, (1979).

Hewitt, Martin, and Poole, Robert. (eds.), *The Diaries of Samuel Bamford,* Sutton Publishing Ltd, Stroud, (2000).

Hill, C. P. *British Economic History and Social History 1700-1982,* Edward Arnold Publishers Ltd, London, (1986).

Hinde, Wendy. *Castlereagh*, Collins, London, (1981).

Hindle, G.B. *Provision for The Relief of The Poor in Manchester 1754-1826,* Manchester University Press, (1975).

Horrocks, Paul. (ed.), *The Making of Manchester*, Manchester Evening News Ltd, Manchester, (1999).

Horton, Harry. *Peterloo, 1819: A Portfolio of Contemporary Documents*, Manchester Libraries Committee, (1969).

Hylton, Stuart. *A History of Manchester*, Phillimore & Co. Ltd, Chichester, (2003).

Jackson, Thomas Alfred. *Trials of British Freedom*, Lawrence and Wishart, London, (1940).

Kennedy, Michael. *Portrait of Manchester*, (The Portrait Series), Robert Hale & Co., London, (1970).

Kidd, Alan. *Manchester*, (third edition), Edinburgh University Press, Edinburgh, (2002).

Konstam, Angus. *Historical Atlas of The Napoleonic Era*, Mercury Books, London, (2003).

Leighton, Margaret, E. *Peterloo Monday, 16th August 1819: A Bibliography*, Manchester Libraries Committee, Manchester, (1969)

Lynch, Michael, *Nineteenth-Century British History 1800-1914*, Hodder and Stoughton, London, (2005).

Marlow, Joyce. *The Peterloo Massacre*, Rapp and Whiting, London, (1970).

Marshall, Dorothy. *Industrial England 1776-1851*, Routledge and Kegan Paul, London, (1982).

Martin, Howard. *Britain in the 19th Century*, Thomas Nelson and Sons Ltd. Cheltenham, (1996).

Messinger, Gary, S. *Manchester in the Victorian Age*, Manchester University Press, Manchester, (1985).

O'Brien, Patrick and Quinault, Roland. *The Industrial Revolution and British Society,* Cambridge University Press, (1993).

Pellew, George. *The Life and Correspondence of H. Addington, Viscount Sidmouth*, London, (1847).

Perkin, Harold. *The Origins of Modern English Society 1780-1880*, Routledge and Kegan Paul, London, (1976).

Pimlott, Joe. *The Life and Times of Sam Bamford*, Neil Richardson, Manchester, (1991).

Plumb, J. H. *England In The Eighteenth Century 1714-1815*, Penguin Books Ltd, Harmondsworth, (1965).

Prentice, Archibald. *Historical Sketches and Personal Recollections of Manchester, Intended to Illustrate the Progress of Public Opinion from 1792 to 1832*, Charles Gilpin, Manchester, (1851).

Priestly, J. B. *The Prince of Pleasure and his Regency 1811-20*, Heineman, London, (1969).

Read, Donald. *Peterloo: The 'Massacre' and its Background*, Manchester University Press, Manchester, (1957).

Read, Donald. *The English Provinces c.1760-1960 a study in influence*, Edward Arnold Publishers Ltd, London, (1964).

Redford, Arthur. *The History of Local Government in Manchester*, Longmans Green and Co. London, (1940).

Reid, Robert. *The Peterloo Massacre*, Heineman, London, (1989).

Ridings, Elijah. *Streams From An Old Fountain*, John Heywood, Manchester, (1863).

Ridings, Elijah. *The Volunteers: or An Englishman's Domestic View of His Political Position*, Manchester, (1860).

Ridings, Elijah. *The Wanderers, or The Wailings of The Outcasts*, John Heywood, Manchester, (1856).

Ridings, Elijah. *The Village Muse, Containing The Complete Works of Elijah Ridings,* (third edition), Thomas Stubbs, Macclesfield, (1854).

Ridings, Elijah. *The Village Festival*, Manchester, (1848).

Smelser, Neil, J. *Social Change In The Industrial Revolution, An Application of Theory to the Lancashire Cotton Industry 1770-1840*, Routledge and Kegan Paul Ltd, London., (1972).

Schama, Simon. *Britain The Fate of Empire 1776-2000*, BBC Worldwide Ltd, London, (2000).

Speck, W.A. *A Concise History of Britain 1707-1975*, Cambridge University Press, Cambridge, (1995).

Stamp, A.H. *A Social and Economic History of England from 1700 to 1970*, Research Publishing Co, London, (1979).

Stevenson, J. *Popular Disturbances in England 1700-1870*, Longman, London, (1992).

Strong, Roy, Sir. *The Story of Britain*, Fromm International Publishing Corporation, New York, (1997).

Swindles, T. *Manchester Streets and Manchester Men*, (fifth Series), J.E. Cornish Ltd, Manchester, (1908).

The Concise Dictionary of Biography From earliest times to 1985, Oxford University Press, (1995).

Trevelyan, George Macaulay. *British History in the Nineteenth Century and After, 1782-1919,* Longmans Green and Co., London, (1922).

Thomis, Malcolm, I. *The Luddites, Machine-Breaking in Regency England*, David and Charles Publishers, Newton Abbot, (1970).

Thompson, E.P. *The Making of the English Working Class,* Victor Gollancz, London, (1963).

Thompson, E.P. *The Making of The English Working Class*, Penguin Books Ltd, London, (1991).

Thompson, E.P. *Making History: Writings on History and Culture*, The New York Press, New York, (1994).

Turner, Michael, J. *British politics in an age of reform*, Manchester University Press, Manchester, (1999).

Turner, Michael, J. *Reform and Respectability: The Making of Middle-Class Liberalism in early nineteenth-century Manchester*, Chethams Society, Carnegie Publishing Ltd, Lancaster, (1995).

Walton, John, K. *Lancashire a Social History, 1538-1939*, Manchester University Press, (1987).

Waghorn, Tom. 'Killing Field,' in Horrocks, Paul, (ed.), *The Making of Manchester*, Manchester Evening News Ltd, Manchester, (1999).

Warmsley, Robert. *Peterloo: The Case Re-Opened*, Manchester University Press, Manchester, (1969).

Wickwar, William Hardy. *The struggle for freedom of the press, 1819-1832*, George Allan and Unwin Ltd., (1928).

Williams, Glyn, and Ramsden, John. *Ruling Britannia A Political History of Britain 1688-1988*, Longman, London, (1990).

White, Reginald James. *Waterloo to Peterloo*, Penguin Books, London, (1957).

Woodward, Llewellyn, Sir. *The Age of Reform 1815-1870*, (second edition), The Clarendon Press, Oxford, (1962).

Journal Articles

Clayson, Jim. 'The Poetry of Peterloo,' *Manchester Regional History Review*, Vol. iii, (1989), pp. 31-38.

Bee, Malcolm and Walter. 'The Casualties of Peterloo,' *Manchester Regional History Review*, iii, (1989), pp. 43-50.

Belchem, John. 'Henry Hunt and the evolution of the mass platform,' *English Historical Review*, xciii, (1978), pp. 766-7.

Belchem, John. 'Manchester, Peterloo and The Radical Challenge,' *Manchester Regional History Review*, Vol. iii, (1989), pp. 9-14.

Bush, Michael. 'Richard Carlile and the Female Reformers of Manchester,' *Manchester Regional History Review*, Vol. xvi, (1989), pp. 2-12.

Bush, Michael. 'The Women at Peterloo: the Impact of Female Reform on the Manchester Meeting of 16 August 1819,' *History*, 89, (2004), pp. 209-32.

De Motte, Margaret. ' Peterloo Revisited,' *Manchester Regional History Review*, Vol. iii, (1989), pp. 76-81.

Donald, Diana. 'The Power of Print: Graphic Images of Peterloo,' *Manchester Regional History Review*, Vol. iii, (1989), pp. 21-30.

Hall, Catherine. 'The Great Reform Act,' *BBC History*, Vol. 8, No. 8, August, (2007), pp. 50-53.

Hunt, Tristram. 'No Marx without Engels,' *History Today*, Vol. 59, April, (2009), pp. 48-51.

Kirk, Neville. 'Commonsense, Commitment and Objectivity: Themes In The Recent Historiography of Peterloo,' *Manchester Regional History Review*, Vol. iii, (1989), pp. 61-66.

Lawson, Philip. 'Reassessing Peterloo,' *History Today*, Vol. March, (1988), pp. 24-29.

Lawson, Philip, 'Peterloo: A Costables Eye-View Re-Assessed,' *Manchester Regional History Review*, Vol. iii, (1989).

Marlow, Joyce. 'The Day of Peterloo,' *Manchester Regional History Review,* Vol. iii, (1989), pp. 3-7.

Poole, Robert. 'The March To Peterloo: Politics and Festivity In Late Georgian England,' *Past and Present*, No. 192. August, (2006).

Read, Donald. Review of 'Peterloo: The Case Reopened, by Robert Walmsley,' *History*, Vol. 55, (1970), pp. 138-40.

Sellers, Ian. 'Prelude To Peterloo: Warrington Radicalism, 1775-1819,' *Manchester Regional History Review*, Vol. iii, (1989), pp. 15-20.

Sheffield, Gary. 'Wellington's Mastery,' *BBC History*, Vol. 8, No. 7, July (2007), pp. 14-19.

Thompson, E. P. 'God and King and Law,' *New Reasoner*, 3, (1957-8).

Thompson, E. P. 'Thompson on Peterloo,' *Manchester Regional History Review*,' Vol. iii, (1989), pp. 67-75.

Tomlinson, V.I. 'Postscript to Peterloo,' *Manchester Regional History Review*,' Vol. iii, (1989), pp. 51-60.

Trevelyan, G.M. 'The number of Casualties at Peterloo,' *History*, V11, (1922), pp. 209-32.

Select Bibliography

Essential reading for the historian must be Samuel Bamford's *Passages in the Life of a Radical* (1844), followed by F.A. Bruton's *The Story of Peterloo,* Manchester, (1919), appearing in the year of the centenary of Peterloo, followed by his *Three Accounts of Peterloo, by Eyewitnesses, Bishop Stanley, Lord Hylton, Benjamin Smith*, Manchester, (1921). Both works are considered as standard modern authorities. Bruton's *Short History of Manchester and Salford,* (1924), contains an account of his *Story of Peterloo* condensed into a few pages. As early as 1922 G.M. Trevelyan published his article, '*The Number of Casualties at Peterloo,*' in *History*, Volume, VII, (1922), in which he presents an incomplete list of the casualties of Peterloo, and urges further research on the subject. Essential reading also is Archibald Prentice, *Historical Sketches and Personal Recollections of Manchester, Intended to Illustrate the Progress of Public Opinion from 1792 to 1832*, (1851), which records what he heard and saw on the day. Donald Read's, study *Peterloo: The 'Massacre' and its Background*, (1957), is a more detailed study of the background to Peterloo and is more exhaustive than any published previously, but does not contain eyewitness accounts. The 150th anniversary of the Peterloo witnessed the appearance of three new publications. The first by Harry Horton, *Portfolio of Contemporary Documents,* Manchester Libraries Committee, (1969), a well presented folder of plans, prints, and broad-sheets. The second was Joyce Marlow's, *The Peterloo Massacre*, (1969), called by the publisher 'the first book for the general reader.' The third, right wing, interpretation was Robert Warmsley's book, *Peterloo:*

The Case Re-opened, Manchester, (1969). Soon afterwards Donald Read's Review of 'Peterloo: The Case-Reopened, by Robert Walmsley,' appeared in *History*, Vol. 55, (1970). The 170th anniversary of Peterloo witnessed the appearance of Robert Reid's popular account, *The Peterloo Massacre*, London, (1989), followed by a collection of essays published in the *Manchester Regional History* Review, Volume, III, (1989), containing essays by Jim Clayson, on *The Poetry of Peterloo*, John Belchem, *Manchester, Peterloo and The Radical Challenge*; Philip Lawson, *Peterloo: A Constables Eye-View Re-assessed*; Margaret De Motte, *Peterloo Revisited*, Diana Donald, *The Power of Print: Graphic Images of Peterloo*; Neville Kirk, *Commonsense, Commitment And Objectivity: Themes In The Recent Historiography of Peterloo*; E.P. Thompson's article from *The Times Literary Supplement* of 11th December (1969) appears in this collection under the heading *Thompson on Peterloo*. Joyce Marlow writes *The Day of Peterloo*, followed by Ian Sellers on *Prelude To Peterloo: Warrington Radicalism, 1775-1819*; V.I. Tomlinson, *Postscript To Peterloo*; Malcolm and Walter Bee, *The Casualties of Peterloo*. This was followed by Michael Bush, 'The Women at Peterloo: the Impact of Female Reform on the Manchester Meeting of 16 August 1819,' *History*, 89, (2004). More recently Michael Bush has produced his splendid book *The Casualties of Peterloo*, Lancaster, (2005), in which he provides detailed listings of every known casualty and his analyses of these lists establishes the true scale and nature of the massacre. Robert Poole 'By the Law or the Sword: Peterloo Revisited,' *History*, xci. (2006), Robert Poole, 'The March To Peterloo: Politics And

Present, No. 192. August, (2006). Most histories of 19th Century Britain make some reference to Peterloo in their indexes.

Index